THE PURE
CONCEPT OF
DIPLOMACY

Recent Titles in
Global Perspectives in History and Politics
George Schwab, Editor

This is a Subseries to Contributions in Political Science.

THE PURE CONCEPT OF DIPLOMACY

José Calvet De Magalhães

Translated by Bernardo Futscher Pereira

Contributions in Political Science, Number 214

GLOBAL PERSPECTIVES IN HISTORY AND POLITICS

GREENWOOD PRESS
NEW YORK • WESTPORT, CONNECTICUT • LONDON

JX
1662
.M28
1988

Library of Congress Cataloging-in-Publication Data

Magalhães, José Calvet De, 1915–
[Diplomacia pura. English]
   The pure concept of diplomacy / José Calvet De Magalhães ;
translated by Bernardo Futscher Pereira.
      p. cm.—(Contributions in political science, ISSN 0147–1066 ;
no. 214. Global perspectives in history and politics)
   Translation of: A diplomacia pura.
   Bibliography: p.
   Includes index.
   ISBN 0–313–26259–4 (lib. bdg. : alk. paper)
   1. Diplomacy.   2. International relations.   I. Title.
II. Series: Contributions in political science ; no. 214.
III. Series: Contributions in political science.   Global
perspectives in history and politics.
JX1662.M2813   1988
327.2—dc19   88–3109

British Library Cataloguing in Publication Data is available.

Library of Congress Catalog Card Number: 88–3109
ISBN: 0–313–26259–4
ISSN: 0147–1066

First published in 1988

Greenwood Press, Inc.
88 Post Road West, Westport, Connecticut   06881

Printed in the United States of America

The paper used in this book complies with the
Permanent Paper Standard issued by the National
Information Standards Organization (Z39.48–1984).

10 9 8 7 6 5 4 3 2 1

It is generally better to deal by speech than by letter; and by the mediation of a third man than by a man's self.

Francis Bacon, *Of Negotiating, Essays*

CONTENTS

INTRODUCTION

LACK OF PRECISION IN THE USE OF THE TERMS "FOREIGN POLICY" AND "DIPLOMACY"

The theory of international relations is still a young and little developed science, which unfortunately, in our opinion, has often strayed into arid paths, using highly sophisticated techniques that make its diffusion and assimilation by the public at large difficult. On the other hand, as we shall see, the theory of foreign policy as such has not received much theoretical attention. As a result, in current language and even in the works of scholars of international affairs, a certain conceptual confusion persists, making it difficult to approach with clarity any theoretical matter pertaining to international relations. In particular the concept of foreign policy, which is of special interest to us at this point, is frequently confused with the concept of international politics on the one hand, and that of diplomacy on the other. Furthermore, the term diplomacy is used without any theoretical rigor to designate different things. Sometimes it is used as a synonym of foreign policy, but often also to signify the peaceful and generic instrument of foreign policy—that is, any form of negotiation—as opposed to violent instruments, and in particular to war.

Scholars of international relations commonly confuse the concepts of foreign policy and diplomacy, sometimes consciously and deliberately. As an example, we can quote a scholar of international politics at the University of Wales, who says the following in the introduction of an interesting work about diplomacy in modern European history, which he edited: "The word diplomacy in the title of this volume is used not in its narrower sense of the professional work of a diplomat but in its wider reference to the full range of international politics as in the familiar phrase 'diplomatic history.' "

In fact, most or almost all writings devoted to "diplomatic history" do not deal with the history of diplomacy as such but rather with the history of foreign relations or of the foreign policy of certain countries.

In his famous work *War and Peace Among Nations*, the well-known sociologist Raymond Aron begins by defining diplomacy as a method of conducting relations among states (a peaceful method, contrasting with the violent method that he calls strategy), but he then uses the word diplomacy to mean foreign policy, as, for example, when he says, referring to the policy of the balance of power: "Hateful or admirable, woeful or precious, the diplomacy of the balance of power results not from the deliberate choice of statesmen but rather from the circumstances with which they are faced." However, the policy of the balance of power can be carried out either by diplomacy or by strategy, to use Aron's own terms. On the other hand, when he considers diplomacy as a peaceful instrument of foreign policy, Aron follows a general tendency to identify diplomacy with negotiation, that is, with all the peaceful methods of conducting relations among states. As we shall see more clearly further ahead, this is a simplistic conception, because it uses the same word to mean essentially distinct concepts or processes.[1]

In the same fashion, Hans J. Morgenthau, one of the pioneers of the theory of international politics in the United States, in his classic work *Politics Among Nations*, treats diplomacy as if it were identical with foreign policy, whenever the object of that policy is to assure peace among nations through the "accommodation" of their respective interests.[2]

The identification between diplomacy and foreign policy is so frequent and persistent that it sometimes leads to unexpected conclusions. Thus, for example, we find in a study (published in 1973 under the title *Peace and War* that was carried out by Colgate University—an American school specializing in international studies—a chapter with the bizarre title: "War and Deterrence as Instruments of Diplomacy."[3] Here war, which, like diplomacy, is an instrument of foreign policy, appears as an instrument of diplomacy, which is not the most appropriate way to clarify and define concepts. This lack of rigor in the use of the terms foreign policy and diplomacy even leads to unfortunate twistings of certain classic statements, as is the case with Clausewitz's famous statement that "war is the simple continuation of politics by other means,[4] which in the aforementioned study is attributed to Clausewitz in the following form: "War is the simple continuation of diplomacy by other means."[5] Clausewitz not only never used the word diplomacy in his widely quoted definition of war but rather asserted when explaining his concept that "War is not just a political act but a true political instrument, a way of conducting political relations, a consummation of these by other means."[6] Clausewitz's thought is therefore quite clear, and to substitute the word politics for diplomacy in his text serves only to create a deplorable confusion.

In the same study carried out by Colgate University, there also appears a transcription of an excerpt of a work by Thomas Schelling, considered one of the most notable American theoreticians of strategy, with the title, strange in itself, *Diplomacy of Violence*, in which it is said that diplomacy is bargaining. This is acceptable in principle because in this case diplomacy is considered an instrument. However, in developing his concept of war, Schelling distinguishes between the use of force and the threat of force and emphasizes that the possibility of doing harm, of destroying, can be used as a negotiating lever in order to conclude that "the power to hurt is bargaining power. To exploit it is diplomacy—vicious diplomacy, but diplomacy."[7] Probably without noticing, in the space of one or two pages, Schelling passes from the concept of diplomacy as a political instrument using negotiation, which is a purely peaceful method, to the political instrument of the threat of force, which cannot be held to be a peaceful method of conducting relations between peoples. Schelling even speaks of coercive diplomacy, which uses violent acts in order to instill in the adversary the fear of even more violent acts that may follow. Although diplomacy, as an instrument of foreign policy, may use several methods (including threats that do not imply the use of force, made precisely in order to avoid recourse to it), when these threats do imply the use of force, we have entered the field of military pressure and left that of diplomacy as a peaceful means to solve conflicts among nations. Thus, it would be more appropriate to speak of coercive policy rather than coercive diplomacy, an expression that inevitably will lead to conceptual confusions. But scholars of international relations are so attracted by the word diplomacy that they cannot resist the temptation to use it even when we leave the field of peaceful means for that of violent ones.

This temptation for the indiscriminate use of the word diplomacy is so strong and so deeply rooted that even experts in diplomacy do not avoid it, confusing diplomacy with foreign policy. Thus the late professor of history at Columbia University, Garrett Mattingly, author of one of the most remarkable historical studies about diplomacy, entitled *Renaissance Diplomacy*, in which diplomatic activity is studied with great depth and accuracy, ends up often using the term diplomacy to mean foreign policy, and therefore feels the need to adopt the expression "diplomatic machinery" to designate diplomacy proper.[8]

Most surprising, however, is that Harold Nicolson, a career diplomat and a remarkable writer who dedicated several studies to diplomatic theory, after vehemently denouncing the confusion between diplomacy and foreign policy in his well-known essay *Diplomacy* (first published in 1939), ends up unwittingly confusing the two in several passages, both in the aforementioned essay and in another book (published in 1954) called *The Evolution of Diplomatic Method*.[9]

If we leave the field of experts in international relations and enter that of non-experts, namely journalists, the conceptual confusion in the matter we are examining is complete, which no doubt is more readily excusable than the confusion—deliberate or not—among scholars of international relations. The well known newspaper *Le Monde*, for example, publishes a section entitled *Diplomatie* that is clearly devoted to certain events in the field of foreign policy. Examples such as these could be multiplied *ad nauseum.*

However, not everything is negative in this matter of delimiting the concepts of foreign policy and diplomacy. An encouraging event is the recent (1978) creation in Georgetown University of an Institute for the Study of Diplomacy, which was established to call attention to the key role of diplomacy, to distinguish it from foreign policy, and to develop the study of diplomacy as an instrument for implementing foreign policy. In the brochure describing the activities of the Institute, it is said that "most scholars, commentators and institutions dealing with foreign relations have failed to distinguish adequately between 'foreign policy' and 'practical diplomacy,' usually slighting the latter." And, it is added: "There is thus a surprising—and distressing—lack of teaching and research materials on the subject of diplomacy. . . . Nowhere is there a broadly gauged textbook or series of case studies that explain and analyze how the diplomatic process works and why it works well or badly in certain situations." According to the same brochure, the Institute wishes to devote itself to the study of the diplomatic process as a distinct matter from the process of formulating foreign policy, conceiving diplomacy as "the means by which countries seek to achieve the ends of their foreign policy by agreement rather than war." As we have already said, it is a hopeful attempt to eliminate the confusion so often found among theoreticians of international politics between foreign policy and diplomacy, in order to render autonomous the theoretical study of the latter. The Institute has already produced some valuable studies and we hope that in the future it will fully achieve its goals.

On the other hand, some recent textbooks from U.S. universities treat diplomacy as an instrument of foreign policy, something which already shows a tendency to use the term diplomacy in its exact sense.[10]

REASONS FOR THIS LACK OF PRECISION

At this point it is pertinent to ask ourselves why scholars of international relations, in spite of all their concern for theoretical rigor, continue to use the word diplomacy to designate the concept of foreign policy, since this latter term is perfectly clear in and of itself and perfectly suited to the concept it wishes to express—certainly more so than the term diplomacy, which historically specifically designated the activities of diplomats or diplomatic agents, and for which, moreover, no substitute term or expression is available. Why confuse different concepts by using one and the same word for both? If, in the aforementioned books by Professor Martin and Professor Aron, we change the quoted passages by replacing the word *diplomacy* with the term *foreign policy*, their meaning would not be altered at all but would rather become clearer.

There are certain bad habits to which even the most renowned theoreticians fall prey and that are difficult to combat once they become engrained. In this particular case, the responsibility lies in great part with the already mentioned fact that the recent and still feeble development of the theory of international relations has not yet produced a strong personality that, in a fundamental work, would determine the terminology of this branch of political science. On the other hand, theoretical works about diplomacy proper are unfortunately rare and little developed. Thus, it can be said that so far no scholar of international relations has yet analyzed in depth the concept of diplomacy, which as a result has become confused and mixed up with other concepts.

THE BOUNDING OF THE CONCEPT OF DIPLOMACY AND THE STATE OF ITS THEORETICAL STUDY

It is therefore necessary to define with greater precision some concepts directly or indirectly related to our theme.

Firstly, we must define the concept of foreign policy. It is naturally opposed to the concept of internal policy and, in this sense, it refers to the activity of a state in the external domain, that is, beyond its political boundaries. The expression foreign policy, therefore, is used by us to designate that part of the activity of a state whose object is to achieve a certain result vis-à-vis another state or group of states. From the theoretical point of view, foreign policy is one aspect of international politics. Foreign policy can be defined as the whole set of decisions and actions of a state in the external domain. International politics encompasses the interactions of the different states, so that we can say, in a highly general way, that international politics encompasses the whole set of the different national foreign policies.

Lately, especially since the end of World War II, the theoretical study of international politics has developed considerably, especially due to the efforts of American scholars. However, the theoretical study of foreign policy as such has been somewhat rudimentary, fragmented, and, in most cases, inconclusive. One of the most important theoreticians of international relations is Professor James Rosenau of Rutgers University, who has dealt in particular with the theory of foreign policy. In 1966, in a study called *Pre-Theories and Theories of Foreign Policy*, he said that "foreign policy analysis is devoid of general theory,"[11] and he added: "The nontheoretical state of foreign policy research is all the more perplexing when it is contrasted with developments elsewhere in American political science."[12] Since then, Professor Rosenau and other scholars have produced some works of importance for the study of the theory of foreign policy,[13] which, notwithstanding, continues to be in the state of pre-theory or theoretical approaches.

The object of our work is limited to the theoretical study of one of the instruments and techniques used to implement a given foreign policy. Whereas some of those instruments and techniques have been the object of in-depth theoretical studies, others, such as diplomacy, have not yet received adequate theoretical treatment. On the other hand, global studies about these instruments and techniques are fragmentary and superficial, a deplorable situation, since theoretical constructions about the analysis of foreign policy depend in great part on knowledge of these matters. The terminological and conceptual confusion apparent in the treatment of matters related to foreign policy, some characteristic examples of which were given above, derives, in the last analysis, from the lack of such studies.

GENERAL NOTIONS ABOUT THE INSTRUMENTS
OF FOREIGN POLICY AND THEIR CLASSIFICATION

We alluded to instruments and techniques of foreign policy because the two notions are as intimately related as, for example, organ and function. In current language, *instrument* means the object that serves to perform a given operation, and *technique* or *method* means the process or set of processes used by a science or art, that is, by a given human activity. Therefore, an instrument is the object used to perform a given operation, and technique the process used to perform it. If we pass from the field of material things to that of human institutions, any of those institutions will be called an instrument when it serves to perform a given human activity.

Instrument and technique, therefore, are closely linked, as static and dynamic aspects of the same reality. Thus we can order certain fields of human activity on the basis of the diverse techniques or diverse instruments used in them. Since each of these techniques is closely linked to a given instrument, this ordering can be carried out equally by reference to the instruments or to the techniques used. In the present study, we do not try to dissociate instrument and technique. Rather, our analysis will proceed as if instrument and technique, object and process, formed a whole.

In the implementation of a given foreign policy, we meet at the outset with a fundamental distinction between the available instruments and techniques: on one side are the instruments and techniques of a peaceful character; on the other, those of a violent character. In the first case, the state that wishes to execute a given foreign policy vis-à-vis another state tries to convince the other state; in the second case, the state that executes its foreign policy tries to constrain the other state at the receiving end of that policy. Raymond Aron, in the book already quoted, stresses this duality of instruments and methods of foreign policy when he writes: "Each State lives in relation to other States: while they live in peace, they must, cost what it may, communicate among themselves. Except when they use force, they try to convince each other. When they fight, then try to constrain each other. In this sense, diplomacy can be considered as the art of convincing without resort to force, and strategy the art of winning with the least possible cost."[14]

While the most typical peaceful instrument of foreign policy is diplomacy, its most typical violent instrument is war. The concept of war, however, does not include all possible types of violent means, just as the concept of diplomacy does not encompass all possible peaceful means available to carry out a given external action. In discussing the violent means, Raymond Aron took care to use, in his book, the generic term *strategy* and not *war*, since he refers to other violent means or means that presuppose the use of force, such as, for example, deterrence, which cannot be called war in the exact sense of the term. Concerning the various peaceful instruments, however, he does not take the same precautions, gathering them all under the label of diplomacy, which he opposes to strategy.

Let us analyze the different peaceful means available for use in implementing a given foreign policy. Whenever a state, or a "a political unit," wants to establish relations with another state or another "political unit"—which is the first positive step in the execution of a foreign policy—the first idea that occurs to us is that of contact. For a state to implement a given foreign policy vis-à-vis another state, it needs first of all to establish contact with that state. The functions of the state are performed by the so-called sovereign organs, which, in accordance with the constitutional rules of the state, have several tasks under their jurisdiction, among which is the task of conducting external activities. The competent organ of State A designates the entity that will represent this state in order to establish contact with the representatives of State B. This international contact constitutes, so to speak, the elemental act of foreign policy, the act of establishing international relations, understood as relations between states. This international contact, however, has a certain goal that constitutes the substance of the foreign policy of State A. The goal can be simply the establishment of good neighborly relations, or the setting up of a political and military alliance, or the establishment of commercial intercourse, and so on. These contacts be-

tween states to arrange the resolution of problems of common
or reciprocal interest are generally called negotiations, in the
widest sense of the word and not in its strict and precise
meaning of an effort to compose differences in order to reach
a given agreement, usually in writing, about some specific
problem. Negotiation means, in the former sense, the dialogue
entered into by the two states. Some authors writing in French
use the word *commerce*, and speak of the commerce among
states, meaning simply this dialogue. Both terms, negotiation
and commerce, come from the vocabulary used in material
transactions, which shows the importance this type of transactions have always had in international relations.

It is curious to observe, as a parenthesis, that the departments of the different states whose task is to conduct foreign
policy have adopted different terms to designate the matter
under this responsibility. In Spain, the respective ministry is
called of external matters and in Brazil of external relations,
both quite generic but suggestive terms. In Great Britain, the
same department is called the Foreign Office, which is even
more generic. In France, however, this department is called
the department of foreign affairs or business. In this last example, the generic idea of negotiation, to which we were al-
luding, is reproduced.

It remains for us to ask now: Does the idea of negotiation,
taken in the sense described above, include all the processes
of peaceful contact of a state with another state? The answer
is negative, since negotiation presupposes a reciprocal contact
and implies an idea of plurilateral contact involving representatives of sovereign organs of two or more states (bilateral
when the negotiations take place between two states and multilateral when they take place between more than two states).
But there are peaceful processes, unilateral in character, that
can be used by a state to get in contact with another state, or,
more explicitly, the population of another state. Thus, when a
state engages a specialized firm to publicize in another state
ideas, facts, or arguments designed to make its foreign policy
more acceptable to the population of the other state, it is using a peaceful but purely unilateral instrument. The same could
be said whenever a state sends to another state secret agents

to obtain information not available to the public that may facilitate the implementation of its foreign policy. Obviously, these forms of international contact cannot be included in the concept of negotiation. Therefore, among the peaceful instruments of foreign policy, the reciprocal or plurilateral means must be distinguished from the unilateral ones.

The plurilateral instruments are identified with what is called in ordinary language negotiation, which, then, is often identified with diplomacy. In the concept of negotiation, however, several types must be distinguished:

a) Negotiation undertaken directly by the holders of political power in the states, a type of negotiation that we will call *direct negotiation*.

b) Negotiation undertaken by representatives of the state especially appointed by the sovereign organs of the state, but who are themselves devoid of political power and who are, strictly speaking, diplomatic agents; this type of negotiation we will call *diplomacy*.

c) Negotiation undertaken by representatives or by the holders of political power of a third state who serve as intermediaries between two states, a type of negotiation we will call *mediation*.

This distinction between the diverse types of plurilateral contacts or negotiation between states does not arise simply out of an abstract need to systematize the subject matter. It contains an essential difference between diplomacy—in the rigorous sense in which we use the word—on the one hand, and on the other, the other forms of negotiation. This will become clear further ahead, when we examine in greater depth the concept of diplomacy.

Regarding the unilateral contacts of a peaceful nature serving a given foreign policy, we can distinguish the following:

a) *Propaganda* (some would prefer to call it information) or infiltration of ideas favorable to the foreign policy of a country among the population of another country.

b) *Espionage* (which Anglo-Saxons bashfully refer to as intelligence) performed by secret agents of a state acting in another state for the gathering by illicit or secret means of information useful to its policy.

c) *Economic intervention* by a state in another state through the various means available in the economic field.

d) *Political intervention* by a state through more or less hidden means among the political circles of another state.

Concerning the violent means of foreign policy, the theory of which is more developed and better known, several distinctions must also be made. By violent instruments, we mean those that require resorting to force on the part of a state to impose its will on another state. But there is a certain difference, discernible even in the current life of individuals, between the possibility of using force, the threat of its use, and its effective use. The military attack of a state against another state—that is, war—is naturally the type of violent instrument of foreign policy par excellence. Taking into consideration the different possible forms of the use of force or military power of a state against another state, it is possible to distinguish the following types of violent instruments of foreign policy:

a) *Deterrence*, that is, the capability of one state, by virtue of its military power, to weigh on another state so as to forestall the possibility that it might take a certain attitude or initiative.

b) *Threat of the use of force* made by one state against another state.

c) *Economic war*, that is, the use of economic sanctions by one state against another, which may require the use of military means, such as a blockade.

d) *Military pressure*, that is, the use of military forces by one state for influencing the decisions of another state without, however, attacking it, as for example, general mobilization, military exercises, concentration of troops on the border, and so on.

e) *War*, that is, the attack by the military forces of one state of the territory, military installations, or population of another state.

Summing up, the instruments of foreign policy can be classified in the following manner:

I. Peaceful instruments of foreign policy

  A. Plurilateral contacts or negotiations

    a) Direct negotiation

    b) Diplomacy

    c) Mediation

  B. Unilateral contacts

    a) Propaganda

    b) Espionage

    c) Economic intervention

    d) Political intervention

II. Violent instruments of foreign policy

  A. Deterrence

  B. Threat

  C. Economic war

  D. Military pressure

  E. War

Chapter 1

THE HISTORICAL EVOLUTION OF DIPLOMACY

PREHISTORY AND ORIENTAL ANTIQUITY

To grasp the concept of diplomacy, it is helpful to briefly survey its historical evolution. Diplomacy is an activity whose roots lie deep in the remote history of humankind. Throughout the centuries, it has undergone several vicissitudes and changes, the examination of which allows us to distinguish with greater clarity its permanent and essential features from its fleeting and extrinsic aspects.

The use of representatives by holders of political power to establish contacts of varied nature between two political units dates back to primitive times, in fact, to the time when political organizations appeared. We surely do not have documentation about these matters referring to prehistoric times. However, the Finnish scholar Ragnar Numelin, in a profound and well-documented study published in 1950 about the "diplomacy" of primitive peoples, shows that they had a perfect knowledge of the use of messengers and envoys between the diverse tribes to treat matters of common interest. His research encompassed the primitive peoples of Australia, Asia, Africa, and the Americas. His conclusion is that these peoples had deeply rooted habits of maintaining intertribal relations through the use of messengers or envoys. According to Numelin,

International thought, or anyhow intertribal thought, is as old as the existence of separate independent political communities, whether primitive tribes or ancient city states and empires. . . . Whether the causes of intertribal relations originate in utilitarian considerations or in magic and religious ideas, it seems certain that even savages have need of maintaining peaceful intercourse with each other, a need usually stronger than those retarding tendencies which work for isolation and a hostile attitude towards foreign tribes and peoples. The reasons for the "diplomatic" treatment of messengers and envoys is possibly to be sought in the same idea which determines the attitude of savages towards hospitality and the treatment of strangers on special occasions: messengers and heralds are believed to be in possession, not only of a protecting taboo, but perhaps also of a supernatural power which it would be fatal to violate. The sanctity of the privileges of the primitive envoy is also to be attributed to the characteristics of his mission. But the office and the privileges attached to it originate in the elementary needs of savage societies. Here, as in so many other instances, religion and magic invest with their form and support, as well with their sanctions, the institutions which those needs have created. As we have seen the primitive peoples choose their emissaries with great discrimination from among the leading men and women of the tribe: the latter are often employed for particularly important missions. It is also to be remarked that the primitive diplomats, as a rule, enjoy personal immunity and are even believed to be invested with something like sanctity. They pass freely through hostile territories. Their reception, as well as the delivery of their messages, take place according to a given ceremonial. And I have proposed the hypothesis that the message stick possibly represents an equivalent to the credentials of civilized peoples."[1]

For the period of Oriental antiquity, there are scattered references to the use of intermediaries among the oriental peoples, namely the Egyptians, the Assyrians, the Babylonians, the Hebrews, the Chinese, and the Hindus.

Concerning the Egyptians, there are documents proving the custom of exchanging envoys between the Egyptian pharaohs and neighboring monarchs. Among those documents are the letters of Tell-el-Amarna and the treaty concluded in 1278 B.C. between the pharaoh Ramses II and the king of the Hittites, Hatursi II. They were discovered in 1887–1888 in the palace of Amenophis or Amenotep II (1411–1375 B.C.) in Amarna, the city of ancient Egypt, half way between Menfis and Tebas, which the successor to Amenotep III, the famous Ikhatanon, transformed into the capital of the kingdom. These documents refer to the exchange of envoys between Egypt and Assyria, Babylon and the kingdom of the Hittites.[2]

About the Assyrians, there is a remarkable cuneiform library from the dynasty of the Sargonides, founded by Sargon II (772–705 B.C.) which contains a wealth of documentation about the external activities of Assurbanipal (668–626 B.C.), the last great king of Assyria. In this documentation there are numerous references to envoys of the Assyrian king to the neighboring monarchs, especially from Babylon and Elam.[3]

The annals of ancient China testify equally to the existence of protocol rules to be applied in relations among the different nations, in spite of the fact that the Middle Kingdom, always very isolationist, was not keen on stimulating external contacts.[4]

In the *Laws of Manu*, one of the pillars of Hindu civilization, dating back to the third century B.C., there are important references to the use of intermediaries between countries. There is even the following statement about the usefulness of diplomacy: "Peace and its opposite (that is war) depend on the ambassadors, since it is they who create and undo alliances. The affairs that provoke war or peace between kings are in their power." In the political treatise *Arthasastra*, by Kautylia, minister of king Chandragupta (322–298 B.C.), there is a chapter about envoys, whose functions are described in the following manner: a) transmitting the points of view of their governments; b) preserving treaties; c) defending the objectives of their state, if necessary by threats, by spreading dissension, by creating secret organizations, by gathering intelligence about the movement of spies, by rendering void treaties unfavorable to their state, by winning over the officials of the host country; d) gathering all information about military installations, wealth, and so on, of the host country.[5]

The most significant references about the use of intermediaries or negotiators in ancient oriental documents are perhaps to be found in the historical books of the Old Testament, especially in the books of Judges, Samuel I and II, Kings I and II, Maccabeus (in the Apocrypha), comprising the period from the thirteenth century to the third century B.C.

Although these books refer much more frequently to the use of violence and military strategy when they relate the relations of the Hebrew people with the other peoples, they nevertheless mention a few instances in which the Hebrews resorted to negotiation, through the use of messengers or envoys.

The book of Judges, for example, mentions that Jepta sent messengers to negotiate with Amnonites[6] and in the book of Samuel, it is said that Abner, who controlled the house of Saul, sent messengers to David to negotiate and bring to an end the differences between the houses of Saul and David.[7]

In Kings II, there is a very interesting and significant reference to a messenger from the Assyrian king Sennacherib (705–681 B.C.) sent to the king of Judea Hezekiah (716–687 B.C.) to propose to him his submission to the king of Assyria. It cannot be said that this messenger, a high official from the court of the Assyrian king, was a negotiator or a messenger of peace, since his mission was to intimidate or constrain the king of Judea, urging him to submit to his sovereign by invoking his greater military power. This was a case of true military pressure and not of diplomacy or negotiation. The words attributed by the book of Kings to the Assyrian envoy, however, are of the greatest interest because they oppose the method of negotiation, on the one hand, to the military method, on the other, naturally proclaiming the superiority of the latter. The speech of the Assyrian messenger to the representatives of the king of Judea who went out to meet him begun thus: "Say to Hezekiah: 'Thus speaks the great king, the king of Assyria: What makes you so confident? Do you think empty words are as good as strategy military strength?"[8]

These words denote recognition of the existence of a duality of political instruments: negotiation, or the "empty words," in the speech of the Assyrian, and the use of military force, that is the antinomy between peace and war referred to in the *Laws of Manu*.

GREECE

Evidence about the use of envoys or intermediaries between the different political units becomes more abundant and elucidating at the time of classical antiquity.

Greek history, in particular, provides clear examples of the widespread use of intermediaries, who were sent from one city to another to take care of the interests of their respective lands.

These intermediaries, who are called ambassadors in modern translations, were persons of high standing, socially eminent, and, therefore, generally of advanced age. The Greek word for envoy or ambassador was *presbeis*, generally used in the plural, since in the Greek system the embassies or missions were collective. In the singular, the word was *presbeutês*, derived from *presbus*. But this word is used in the singular only by the older writers, such as Aeschylus or Aristophanes.[9] These words, *presbeis* or *presbeutês*, meant "important person," "leading man," and were associated also with the idea of ancientness and thus with the privileges attached to it. An embassy, that is a mission carried out by *presbeis*, was a *presbeia*, meaning "a mission of noteworthy or venerable people."[10]

In Athens, the envoys were chosen by the people, in principle by all the Athenians. Sometimes, however, the Senate, by special delegation, chose part or all of the members of the mission. In Sparta, the choice of envoys was made by the *ephors*, the magistrates who presided over the assembly. In Sparta, each mission was composed usually of three envoys. In Athens, the number was usually three, five, or ten envoys. In Athens, the foreign envoys presented themselves before the Senate. They were met first by the *prytanis*, the delegation from the Senate. They presented their credentials at this moment and explained the nature of their mandate. The Senate then presented the envoys to the Assembly of the people, to whom they explained once again the nature of their mandate. They were then questioned and a debate or discussion followed, at the end of which the envoys withdrew in order for the Assembly to proceed to voting. The answer of the Assembly was then communicated to them.[11]

Because of the procedure described, the envoys had to possess qualities of oratory and therefore were often chosen from among the most reputed speakers of a city. Whence the designation of *orator* applied to these envoys in Roman times, together with the designations *legatus* and *nuntius*, as we shall see.

One of the main sources for the study of the system of intermediaries or ambassadors in ancient Greece is certainly Thucydides (460–399 B.C.). In his *History of the Peloponnesian War*, he often refers to envoys and emissaries sent by one of the Greek city-states to another to care for matters of common or reciprocal interest, usually to celebrate pacts of alliance, since the Greek cities were often involved in struggles for hegemony.

Envoys or ambassadors are frequently mentioned throughout Thucydides' book. Thus, during the dispute (which resulted in the Peloponnesian War) between Corcira and Corinthus over Epidamus, a colony of the former city, in the fifth century B.C., both cities tried to gain the support of Athens by sending ambassadors to that city in the year 438 B.C. The envoys of both were heard by the Athenian Assembly, where they made long speeches defending their respective causes. The Assembly then met in closed session to deliberate over the course to be taken.[12]

Around the year 445 B.C., Corinthus and some of its allies sent ambassadors to Sparta to complain about the abuses committed by Athens and to convince the Lacedaemonians to declare war on the Athenians. The envoys addressed the Assembly; the last one to speak was a representative of Corinthus who made an eloquent speech prodding the Spartans to action.[13] Thucydides reports:

But there happened to be present at Lacedaemon an embassy of the Athenians that had come on other business and when they heard the various speeches they deemed it advisable to appear before the Lacedaemonians, not indeed to make any defence on the charges brought by the cities, but to make clear with regard to the whole question at issue that the Lacedaemonians should not decide it hastely but should take more time to consider it.[14]

Having asked to be heard in the Assembly, their demand was granted, and after their speech the Assembly met again to deliberate. In the end, a majority emerged opposed to the Athenians and favorable to a declaration of war against Athens. The king of the Lacedaemonians, Arquidamus, who was, according to Thucydides, "a man reputed to be both sagacious and prudent" then made a speech, to which Harold Nicolson called attention because of the argument made in it that negotiation should be used before embarking on a military enterprise.[15]

After analyzing the military capabilities of Sparta and Athens and the consequences of a long and generalized war, Arquidamus states:

Yet assuredly I do not advise you that you should blindly suffer them to injure our allies and allow their plotting to go undetected, but rather that you should adopt the following course: Do not take arms yet, but send envoys to them and make complaints, without indicating too clearly whether we shall go to war or put up with their conduct; also in the meantime, let us proceed with our own preparations, in the first place by winning allies to our side, Barbarians as well as Hellenes, in the hope of obtaining from some quarter or other additional resources in ships or money (for those who, like ourselves, are plotted against by the Athenians are not to be blamed if they procure their salvation by gaining the aid, not of Hellenes only, but even of Barbarians); and let us at the same time be developing our resources at home. And if they give any heed to our envoys, there could be nothing better; but if not, then, after the lapse of two or three years, we shall at length be better equipped to go against them, if we decide to do so. Or perhaps when they see our preparations, and that our words correspond thereto, they will be more inclined to yield, for they will both have their land still unravaged and their deliberations will concern goods that are still theirs and as yet not ruined. For do not regard their land as anything but a hostage for us to hold, and a better hostage the better it is cultivated. You should therefore spare it as long as possible, instead of making them desperate and thus having a more intractable foe to deal with. For if, without adequate preparation, egged on by the complaints of our allies, we shall ravage their territory, beware lest we adopt a course which might rather result in disgrace and difficulties for the Peloponnesus. For complaints, indeed, whether brought by states, or by individuals, may possibly be adjusted; but when a whole confederacy, for the sake of individual interests, undertakes a war of which no man can foresee the issue, it is not easy to conclude it with honour. And let no man think it pusillanimous that many states should hesitate to attack a single city. For they also have allies not less numerous than ours who pay tribute; and war is a matter not so much of arms as of money, for it is money alone that makes arms serviceable, especially when an island opposes a maritime power. Let us therefore provide ourselves with money first, instead of being carried away prematurely by the eloquence of our allies; and, just as it is we who shall bear the greater part of the responsibility for the consequences, whether for good or evil, so let it be our task also calmly to get some forecast of them. And so be not ashamed of the slowness and dilatoriness for which they censure us most; for speed in beginning may mean delay in ending, because you went into the war without preparation.[16]

And, concluding, Arquidamus says:

And send envoys to the Athenians to take up the question of Potidaea, and also to take up the matters wherein our allies claim that they are wronged. The chief reason for this is that they are ready to submit to arbitration, and it is not lawful to proceed forthwith against one who offers arbitration as though against a wrongdoer. But all the while prepare yourselves for the war. This decision will be best for yourselves and will inspire most fears in your foes.[17]

However, one of the ephors, the high magistrates who presided over the Assembly, insisted on declaring war on the Athenians. The issue was again put to a vote, and the majority chose not to heed the prudent words of King Arquidamus, declaring itself favorable to war. The war of the Peloponnesian and the resultant expansion of Athens resulted from this decision.

Arquidamus' speech, of which we quoted a long passage, is in fact a remarkable example of the defense of negotiation through the use of intermediaries or ambassadors to solve a conflict between neighboring states. The speech even mentions arbitrage, a sophisticated method for solving international disputes that was only recently enshrined in international law. The classical Greeks had, therefore, quite a precise notion of the usefulness of the diplomatic method—that is, of the use of intermediaries to try to solve, through negotiation, the disputes that arose between the different Greek cities and to promote peaceful relations among them. Thucydides, in reproducing at length Arquidamus' speech, is naturally defending the method of negotiation.

Demosthenes (384–322 B.C.), who was appointed ambassador at least twice, also left us an interesting text, in which he accuses another orator, his embassy colleague Esquines, of corruption and treason. This text is a speech called *The Corrupted Embassy*, which describes the duties of an Athenian ambassador.[18] Addressing the judges who heard the case against Esquines, Demosthenes says that an ambassador is responsible:

For his reports . . . for his advice . . . for the instructions received from you . . . for the use of his time, and . . . for his integrity or lack of it in acquitting all his responsibilities. . . . His reports enable you to examine the situation; if they are truthful, you will decide correctly, otherwise the opposite will happen. . . . You think that the ambassador gives the best advice, because . . . you think that he is aware of the goal of his mission; it is, therefore, just, that the ambassador may not be convinced of having given you false and disadvantageous advice. Furthermore, he must have acted in accord with what you told him to say or do and with what you explicitly ordered him to do. . . . He [is] responsible for the use of his time because . . . it often happens that the moments favorable to many great actions last but little; if anyone should voluntarily miss the occasion or give it away to the adversary, he will not get it back again, no matter what he may do. In what concerns integrity or lack of it, . . . to receive money for something harmful to the state is a crime deserving the greatest indignation.[19]

And further along, Demosthenes adds, still on the responsibilities of ambassadors: "In effect, what should ambassadors be responsible for if not for their words? Ambassadors do not command warships, nor territories nor soldiers, nor fortresses (no one entrusts them with such things) but only time and words."[20] Concerning the use of time or opportunities, Demosthenes further adds that wasting opportunities in an oligarchy or tyranny, or in a democracy such as the Athens of his day are not equal crimes:

In the former regimes . . . everything is promptly run by orders. But, among us, the Council must hear a complete account and then

prepare a report . . . ; then the Assembly must be convened . . .
then the authors of the best proposals must defeat their oppo-
nents. . . . When something is decided, . . . time must be allowed
to find the means to execute it. Therefore, one who deprives [us] . . .
of that time, is depriving us not only of time, but . . . of the capacity
to act.[21]

Demosthenes tells us of the special agendas of the Athenian
Assembly to discuss matters concerning ambassadors. The
heralds were the messengers of war and ambassadors the
messengers of peace. In ancient Greece, the office of herald
was a permanent one, while that of ambassador was temporary. On the other hand, the ambassadors were negotiators
with powers to discuss the matters in their charge, while the
heralds were simply messengers, charged only with transmitting messages about military operations.

ROME

Many authors pretend that the Romans were not particularly interested in the art of negotiation, preferring instead
the art of war. Harold Nicolson even says that the Romans
preferred the methods of "the legionary and the road-maker."
He adds, "The Roman contribution to diplomacy is to be sought
for, not in the area of negotiation, but in the area of international law."[22]

We deem this historical view to be somewhat exaggerated,
since the Romans, although they built the greatest empire of
antiquity and although they had remarkable qualities as war-
riors, often resorted to negotiation and were not involved in
more struggles for hegemony with their neighboring peoples
than the Athenians or other peoples of antiquity. The predominance of strategy over negotiation was not, therefore, a typical characteristic of the Romans. As the historical documents
abundantly show, we also find this predominance in the history of the peoples of Oriental antiquity and in those of ancient Greece. However, Rome built the greatest empire of antiquity, and the fame of its legions overshadowed many of its
other activities.

A special tribune, called *Graecostasis*, even existed in Rome, near the Capitol where, according to the Roman polygraph Marcus Terencius Varro (116–27 B.C.), ambassadors from foreign countries and from the provinces awaited their audiences with the Senate. Toward the end of the Republic, a system was adopted, formally authorized by the *Lex Gabinia*, whereby the month of February was reserved for contacts between ambassadors and the Senate. At an unknown date, the *Graecostasis* was transfered to the Forum, near the temple of Saturn. During the Empire, the institution must have fallen by the wayside since no more references to the *Graecostasis* are to be found.[23]

In Rome, the embassies were appointed by the political organ charged with the supreme direction of state policy. During the Roman monarchy, the ambassadors (*legati*) were chosen by the king; in the republican epoch, embassies were appointed by the Senate upon the proposal of the magistrate who presided to this Assembly; in imperial times, the emperor designated the embassies. Following the Greek example, the embassies were, as a rule, collective and composed of ten to twelve ambassadors with one president (*princeps legationis*). The ambassadors were always chosen from among the leading citizens and were treated with all the honors.

The Romans received ambassadors only from countries to which they recognized the *jus legationis*, thus excluding colonies and subject peoples. Ambassadors from friendly countries were received in Rome with great magnificence and lodged in special buildings in the *villa publica*, in the Field of Mars. The lodging was free (*locus*) and they received magnificent gifts and were invited to public shows. The day that the subject matter of their mission was to be treated in the Senate, they were taken to the *Graecostasis* and were then received for an audience with the Senate. After presenting their mandate, they were bidden farewell with all the honors and accompanied to the border by a questor.

Roman authors normally called envoys or ambassadors *legatus* and embassies *legationi*. However, care must be taken to distinguish these *legati*, who were ambassadors from foreign countries, from the municipal or provincial *legati*, who were sent to the Roman Senate as representatives of the cities or of a provincial *consilium*, that is, a diet composed of the representatives of the municipalities of a given province. Still another type of *legatus* was a purely military office occupied by the sub-commanders of the legions.[24]

Simple messengers or message carriers were called *nuntii*.

The terms *legatus* and *nuntius* are abundantly used by Titus Livius, Cicero, and Caesar, which shows the frequent use of negotiators in the relations between Rome and other peoples.[25] Titus Livius, Ovid, and Virgil also use the term *orator* to designate ambassadors, a usage reminiscent of the Greek tradition, transmitted to the Romans, of appointing as ambassadors persons with acknowledged oratory gifts, or even professional speakers, since they had to address political assemblies to defend the cause of their respective countries.[26]

The passages in Caesar dealing with the inviolability of ambassadors are particularly important because they reveal the meaning attributed to that concept at the time. The Romans had sent several emissaries to the Venetos in order to find wheat to buy for their troops. This haughty people inhabiting the coastal areas of Brittany imprisoned some of those envoys. Learning this, Caesar immediately decided to attack the Venetos, accusing them of having commited a heinous crime. In effect, asks Caesar: "Did not they imprison and put to irons the ambassadors, whose functions all nations have always considered sacred and inviolable?"[27] After defeating them, Caesar decided to severely punish the Venetos "so that in the future barbarians be more respectful of the rights of ambassadors" (*jus legatorum*).[28] These passages clearly show that the Romans considered the inviolability of ambassadors a fundamental principle that was part of *jus gentium*, that is of the endowment of civilized peoples, and its violation an unusual crime even among barbarians.

Attempts at direct negotiation, without the use of intermediaries or *legati*, were rare among the Romans, just as they were in ancient Greece. As an illustrative example, we will mention a single case of an attempt at direct negotiation made by Julius Caesar himself when he led the military operations in Galia. The Germans, led by their king Ariovistus, frequently threatened the peoples of Galia by crossing the Rhine. Caesar thought he could persuade Ariovistus to abandon his aggressive policy if he had a personal meeting with him. To arrange it, he sent emissaries to Ariovistus; after difficult negotiations, the two chiefs, having both taken some precautions for fear of an ambush, finally met face to face. They spent the meeting talking past each other, each maintaining his points of view without taking any account of the other's arguments. Naturally, the meeting was a failure, and Caesar sent ambassadors to Ariovistus, who imprisoned them; another war followed, Caesar emerging once again victorious.[29]

THE MIDDLE AGES

The fall of the Roman empire created a new political situation in western Europe not really based on a state-system but rather on feudal landlords more or less dependent on the emperor and the pope. In such a political situation, confused and chaotic for a long time, the use of diplomacy declined. The Byzantine empire, however, made great use of diplomacy, preferring it to war. In the eighth and ninth centuries, the Byzantine emperors frequently sent representatives, usually high court dignitaries, to the pope and to the feudal monarchs, and particularly to Pepin the Short and Charlemagne.[30] According to Harold Nicolson,

Diplomacy became the stimulant rather than the antidote to the greed and folly of mankind. Instead of cooperation, you had disintegration; instead of unity, disruption; instead of reason, you had astuteness; in the place of moral principles, you had ingenuity. Diplomacy in the Middle Ages had a predominantly Italian and indeed Byzantine flavour. It is to this heredity that it owes, in modern Europe, so much of its disrepute.[31]

Harold Nicolson's observations call for two remarks: first, in spite of his vehement and insistent struggle against the usual confusion between diplomacy and foreign policy, in this paragraph Nicolson refers to Byzantine diplomacy in the dual sense of diplomacy and foreign policy; second, Nicolson could have added that Byzantine diplomacy was also transmitted to Russia, the great cultural inheritor of the empire of Byzantium.[32]

There is a detailed report of an embassy sent by emperor Otto I (912–973) to the emperor of Constantinople, Nicephorus, with the goal of obtaining for his son, the future Otto II (955–983) the hand of princess Teophano, the daughter of the preceding emperor. Luidprand, the bishop of Cremona, was charged with this mission. In the report he left to posterity, the ambassador of the western court describes in detail the habits of the court of Constantinople and the arrogant and sometimes insulting fashion in which he was treated. It is a very interesting document that reveals the oriental style of treating the emissaries of foreign countries (a style that has remained intact throughout the centuries). It is composed chiefly of two traits: seeing in every foreigner a spy and feeling the need to humiliate him by stressing the superiority of the country he is visiting.[33] William Thayer, a diplomat who served in Russia and in several oriental countries, also stresses the parallel between Luidprand's experience in Constantinople of the tenth century and many contemporary aspects of the treatment of diplomats in oriental countries.[34]

As the temporal power of the pope increased, the Church came to utilize mostly the system of representation previously used by the secular authorities. The intricate relations between the popedom and Byzantium led to the creation of an almost permanent papal representation in Constantinople. This representation was assured by officials who were defined as "envoys" or "in charge of a mission" and who were called *apocrisiaries*, which etimologically means "responsible." According to some authors, Rome sent apocrisiaries to the Byzantine court since the fourth century A.D. However, other authors say that those representatives appeared only towards the middle of the fifth century, at the time of Pope Leo (Leo Magnus, 440–461), the emperor being Martianus (450–457). Still others maintain that the institution appeared only at the time of Emperor Justinian (483–565), more precisely in the year 536, when the Byzantine general Belisarius conquered Rome. However, there seems to be no doubt that the institution already existed in the fifth century.[35] The time of the greatest splendor of the Roman apocrisiary in Constantinople was from the middle of the sixth century to the middle of the seventh century. The Church of Rome also maintained apocrisiaries in the court of the Franks from the time of the conversion of Clodoveus or Clovis in 496 and after the preachings of St. Remigius.[36] Concurrently with the existence of these apocrisiaries, the Roman Church also used other representatives who were sent to the imperial court or the councils, and were called *legati*, following the Roman designation. Thus, Pope Liberius (352–366) sent two *legati* to emperor Constantius in the year 353, and others followed the next year. During the papacy of Leo Magnus, several legations left Rome for Constantinople. At the time of Pope Nicholas I (858–867), the papal legates were numerous and enjoyed greater powers. With Gregory VII (1073–1085), a new period of the diplomatic activity of the Church of Rome begun with the sending of numerous legates. Gregory VII defines the legate as a representative of the person of the Bishop of Rome; to designate a legate he also uses the word *nuntius* (*nuntius sedis apostolicae*), equally deriving from Roman tradition, but not in the narrow sense of a simple messenger, as it was used in Roman times.[37]

Like the papal envoys, those of the Christian monarchs kept the Roman designations *legatus* and *nuntius*. In the Merovingian epoch, the title most frequently used was *legatus*, or a variation (*legatarius*, *commisarius*), although *nuntius* and *missus* were also used. The use of *nuntius*, however, became more widespread from the twelfth century onwards, predominating in the thirteenth century, and sharing that predominance from then on with the designations *ambaxator* and *orator*.[38]

The designation *legatus* also continued to be used, but especially for representatives of the pope, together with the designation *nuntius*, as was already mentioned. The canonist Guiglielmo Durandus, in his *Speculum legatorum*, of the thirteenth century, defines *legatus* as the representative of one party sent to another and adds that *nuntii* are also called *legati*.[39] Whereas in Roman times there was a clear distinction in the meaning of the two terms (the envoy and negotiator was called *legatus*, the *nuntius* being simply a messenger), in the Middle Ages, it is difficult to distinguish between one and the other, as is the case with other designations like *procurator*.

This last term was introduced in official language as a result of the revival of Roman law during twelfth century to signify an envoy sent by a monarch to another. The *procurator* was a concept of Roman law corresponding to the legal representative of one person to deal with another and presupposing the existence of a mandate or *plena potestas*. There is evidence that Venetian envoys made use of *plena potestas* in the second half of the twelfth century,[40] and by the end of the century it was commonly used.[41]

Some authors, discussing the differences between the powers of a *nuntius* or *legatus* and of a *procurator* try to show that a *procurator*, because he had *plena potestas*, had powers to conclude negotiations not available to other types of envoys. In truth, however, in the Middle Ages it is difficult to distinguish between a *nuntius* and a *legatus*, and this is also true, in many instances, of the distinction between a *procurator* and a *nuntius* or *legatus*. Thus, many *procuratores* were sent simply to provide explanations, to apologize, or simply to relay messages; and, in some cases, *nuntii* had *plena potestas* and concluded negotiations. Some envoys were called simultaneously *nuntii* and *procuratores*; even in cases in which the representative was clearly a *procurator litis*, he was sometimes designated by the title *nuntius*.[42]

In the medieval era, neither international law nor an international theory were sufficiently developed, and the terminology in these matters was rather imprecise. Even if any distinction between these different designations can be interesting from a legal point of view, it is not very relevant from the point of view of political theory. The important point in all these cases of *nuntius*, *legatus*, *missus*, or *procurator* is that they were intermediaries sent by a holder of political power to another to negotiate. It matters little whether this negotiation was undertaken by an intermediary with powers to initiate it and conclude it, without frequently resorting to the holder of political power, or if it was carried out through successive messages relayed by a simple messenger. The important thing for diplomatic theory is that the negotiation was not directly carried out by the monarchs or by the holders of political power, but by intermediaries. As the medieval canonist Henry de Suze, known as *Hostensis,* observed, not without malice, as long as the intention of the monarch was clear, it mattered little whether the envoy was called an "ass" or anything else.[43]

All these designations for envoys were overtaken by the term *ambassador,* which began to spread in Italy during the thirteenth century. The term ambassador, meaning envoy, is already used in documents of the Milan archives dated 1198 and 1199, but the term came to be more widely used only in the next century. In the arhives of Venice and Genoa, references to ambassadors are frequent in thirteenth-century documents. With the greater use of vernacular languages in medieval documents, several vernacular versions of the Latin term *ambaxiator* or *ambactiator* begun to be adopted. French documents of the twelfth century contain the French form *ambassadeur* or *ambaxateur.* In England, the first known use of the term is attributed to Chaucer, writing around the year 1374.[44]

A great debate took place among the etimologists of the nineteenth century about the etiymology of the words *ambassador* and *embassy,* but no definite conclusion emerged. It is generally admitted that these designations come from the word *ambactus,* of Celtic or German origin, meaning vassal, servant, member of the retinue of a lord. The Roman philologist Sextus Pompeus Festus says in peremptory fashion that *ambactus* in Celtic meant servant.[45] Caesar, speaking about the Celts, says that noblemen had *ambactos et clientes* at their service, which conforms with Festus' opinion.[46] Some authors argue that the Lower Latin term *ambactus* did not derive from the Celtic *ambactus* but from the Gothic *andbahti,* which also meant servant. Almost all the German languages have a similar word. The most correct conclusion seems to us Littré's, who says: "It is difficult to decide between the Celtic and the

German; but doubtlessly in these circumstances as in many others, the Celtic and the German had very close formulations that became entangled in Lower Latin.[47]

In any case, it is certain that in Lower Latin of the initial Middle Ages, there are references to *ambaxia* or *ambactia*. For example, in the *Salic Law*, from the middle of the fifth century, there are references to *ambaxia* in the sense of missions.[48] In a Carolingian document of the year 783, the expression *ambaxiavit* is used to designate the carrying out of a mission.[49] In another document from 877 of Charles the Bald, donating a monastery requested by empress Richildis, the name of the empress appears after the name of the emperor bearing the designation: *Domina Richildis imperatrix ambaxiavit.*[50] This means that the empress intervened in the donation, being charged of a mission connected to it. The designations *ambaxia*, meaning mission, and *ambaxiare*, carrying out a mission, were therefore introduced in Lower Latin by the Germanic peoples, and mysteriously made their way until the end of the twelfth century, when in the Milan archives the term *ambaxiator* is used to signify the person in charge of a mission to a foreign country, as was said above. Evidence that the designation *ambassador* was already current in the thirteenth century and certainly the one preferred by the secular authorities—since *legati* and *nuntii* were adopted particularly by the ecclesiastic authorities—is the fact that in a twelfth-century chronicle (dated precisely from the year 1160), revised in the following century, the word *legati* found in the original text was substituted by the word *ambaxatores.*[51]

In the following centuries, the fourteenth and fifteenth centuries, the term ambassador came to be currently used to designate any envoy, although predominantly to designate envoys sent by secular authorities, the terms legate and nuntio being henceforth reserved for papal envoys. With the Renaissance, the humanists, writing in Latin, temporarily revived the designation *legatus* for envoys of a secular power and also, under the influence of Virgil and Ovid, the designation *orator*, of a more literary flavor. Bernardo du Rosier, writing in 1436 a small treatise in Latin about the role of ambassadors, calls it *Ambaxiator brevilogus, etc.*[52] The influence of humanism, leading to the adoption of terms used in the classic Latin works, was not yet felt in this case. Machiavelli, writing in the year 1514 to his friend Francesco Vittori, appointed ambassador of Florence to the pope, calls him *Magnifico oratori florentino Francisco Vitorio apud Summum Pontifice.*[53] But the humanist Etienne Dolet (1509–1546), who was accused of heresy and burned at the stake in 1546 for having published a translation of Plato, published in Lyon, in the year 1541, a small treatise significantly called *Liber unus de officio legati vulgo ambassiatorem vocant,* that is, "Single Book about the Role of Legates Ordinarily Called Ambassadors."

Until the middle of the seventeenth century, some official documents and in almost all the books written in Latin, the ambassadors are called *legati.*[54] But with the predominance of the vernacular languages, the different forms of the designation ambassador in the different languages became predominant.

Especially from the tenth and eleventh centuries onward, there was an intensification of diplomatic activity, that is, of the use of intermediaries in contacts and negotiations between monarchs and feudal lords. In the last years of the Middle Ages, the use of ambassadors was a common and general practice. The evidence is so abundant that it would be superfluous to quote it. It is sufficient to consult the repositories of medieval documentation to verify this fact.

In the first part of the Middle Ages, from the fifth to the ninth centuries, there were cases of direct negotiation between monarchs, certainly due to the essentially personal character of imperial or royal power. But those direct meetings between the holders of political power did not exclude the use of intermediaries, both to exchange correspondence between heads of state and to prepare and reach agreement in the negotiations themselves; the agreements were then sanctioned by the presence of the monarchs. From the tenth to the twelfth centuries, the number of direct meetings increased. However, in both periods, most negotiations were conducted by envoys representing the respective monarchs.[55]

An experienced diplomat of the transition period between the Middle Ages and the modern period, Philippe de Commynes (1447–1511), noticed the risks and disadvantages of direct meetings between monarchs and spoke eloquently against them in the memoirs that he left us. In these memoirs, which are an important source for French and European history, Commynes devotes a special chapter to the condemnation of direct negotiations between monarchs. In this chapter, he remarks that direct meetings between powerful kings always tend to worsen rather than improve relations between their respective countries, and explains how, underneath the appearances of protocolar niceties, the respective parties amplify and aggravate less positive aspects, with the final result that new feelings of bitterness and resentment arise between the monarchs. He concludes by saying that "great princes should never meet if they want to remain friends."[56] In another frequently quoted passage of his memoirs, Commynes returns to this matter, saying that "two great princes who, in truth, want to enjoy friendly relations should never meet, but rather send each other good and wise men who will compose and rectify whatever is amiss."[57] This bit of wisdom, repeated, as we shall see, throughout the times, seems to have been forgotten in ours, especially in the period following World War II.

THE MODERN AGE

With the birth of the Modern Age, signalled by the maritime discoveries and the Renaissance, the diplomatic institution underwent a profound transformation.

The frequency of contacts between the different Italian political units led to the creation of the resident ambassador. Whereas in antiquity and in the Middle Ages embassies had a temporary character, even when they lasted quite some time, the intense and continued diplomatic activity of the Italian states at the beginning of the modern age created the need for diplomatic representations with a permanent character. Before the end of the fifteenth century, resident ambassadors became a current institution throughout Italy, although one that was practically unknown in the rest of Europe.[58] Although in former times there are sporadic cases of ambassadors staying for a long time in countries to which they were sent, the true creator of the new system of resident ambassadors was the lord of Milan, Giangaleazzo Visconti, who kept a resident ambassador in the court of the Hungarian king and emperor of the Holy Roman Empire Sigismund (1386–1437) for more than seven years, from May 1425 to July 1432.[59] Venice may have kept a permanent ambassador in Milan from 1415 to 1425, when Venice was trying to negotiate peace with Milan. However, the evidence is inconclusive, according to the great historian Garret Mattingly.[60] In 1431, Venice, Florence, and the Popedom allied against Milan, to regain two papal cities conquered by the Milanese, among other things. Just before April 1435, Venice appointed as resident ambassador to Rome the experienced diplomat Zachary Bembo. From 1448 onward, Venice and Florence also exchanged resident ambassadors. In 1457, Naples kept a resident ambassador in Venice and also one in Milan around 1458.[61] In this year, Milan also kept a resident ambassador in Rome. The Popedom received resident ambassadors before sending them to the different Italian courts. During practically all of the fifteenth century, the popes received ambassadors but sent none. After 1495, Alexander VI kept a *nuntius* and *orator* in the court of Emperor Maximilian (1459–1519). Around the year 1500, that same pope appointed permanent representatives to Spain, France, and Venice. In 1506, Jules II (1503–1513) renewed the Popedom's representation in Spain. But the decisive extension of the papal system of permanent diplomatic representation ocurred only in the pontificates of Leo X (1513–1521) and Clement VII (1523–1534). The new institution acquired a precise form after the pontificate of Gregory XIII (1572–1585), attaining its full development at the beginning of the seventeenth century.[62]

However, according to Mattingly, after 1460 Rome was and for a long time continued to be the main school and the main field of diplomatic action. In that city, he wrote, "We find the first signs of something like an organized diplomatic corps, developing a rudimentary sense of professional solidarity."[63]

It was also in Rome that a Venetian diplomat, Ermolao Barbaro (1453–1493), appointed resident ambassador to the papal court in 1490, wrote a small treatise called *De officio legati* about the duties of resident ambassadors.[64] Barbaro was a humanist who taught Aristotle at the University of Padua, the son of a diplomat, and himself an experienced diplomat who had already served in Naples. The small treatise was meant to serve as a guide for one of his friends who wanted to begin a diplomatic career in Venice. In this book, he defines ambassadors as those "who are sent with simple and generic credentials to gain the friendship of princes" and he describes their main duty in the following form: "The first duty of an ambassador is exactly the same as that of any other servant of a government, that is, to do, say, advise and think whatever may best serve the preservation and aggrandizement of his own state."[65]

The system of resident ambassadors spread from Italy to the rest of Europe, although not in a uniform and simultaneous manner. Of all the states competing in the power struggles of late fifteenth century Europe, Spain alone, during the first phase of the Italian wars, created a regular diplomatic service that resembled those established by the main Italian powers after the peace of Lodi in 1454. This was due especially to the personal action of King Ferdinand of Aragon (1452–1516) whose fundamental interest was the hegemonic struggle in Europe, as opposed to his wife, Isabella of Castile, interested mainly in maritime expansion. The diplomatic service installed by Ferdinand of Aragon was, however, quite disorganized, and his ambassadors were often left without instructions and their letters went unanswered.[66]

In 1494, at the time of the invasions of Italy by the French troops of Charles VIII, Maximilian of Austria tried to establish a system of resident ambassadors in Rome, Venice, Milan, England, France, and Spain. In a few years' time, Maximilian's diplomatic system had dissolved entirely because of problems with his allies and financial difficulties that always besieged the emperor.[67]

Henry VII of England (1457–1509) also made a modest attempt to establish a system of permanent embassies. England kept for years a single resident ambassador in Rome. Although Spain was represented in London by a resident ambassador since 1496, an English resident ambassador in Spain was appointed only in 1505. When Henry VIII (1491–1547) acceded to the throne, he increased the diplomatic representation of England, creating permanent embassies in the Low Countries and at the court of the Emperor. Around the year 1520, when the main adviser of Henry VIII, Cardinal Thomas Wolsey (1475–1530), took English foreign policy in his charge, the English system of diplomatic representation was enlarged with resident ambassadors in France and Venice.[68]

In Portugal, the first resident ambassador to Rome was appointed in 1512. In 1521, a Spanish resident ambassador was sent to Lisbon, but only in 1525 was a Portuguese resident ambassador appointed to Madrid. France appointed its first resident ambassador to Lisbon in 1522, and in that same year Portugal sent a resident ambassador to France.[69]

Of all the great European powers of the initial modern period, France took longest to establish a system of permanent diplomatic representation. Francis I (1494–1547), in his hegemonic struggles against the house of Austria, always prefered direct negotiation to diplomacy. This system of negotiation was tried for some time without, however, achieving major results. Let us hear the impartial testimony of the great historian Garrett Mattingly, deeply knowledgeable about the diplomacy of the time:

As the approaching duel between Valois and Habsburg, between Francis I and Charles V, focused the attention of Europe, the normal machinery of diplomatic intercourse yielded to the personal diplomacy of sovereigns. Wolsey's last efforts to save his peace were punctuated by interviews between his master and each of the rival sovereigns. The meeting at the Field of Cloth of Gold of Henry VIII and Francis I was personal diplomacy at its most pompous and spectacular. The two interviews between Henry VIII and Charles V which bracketed and nullified the Anglo-French encounter were personal diplomacy at, perhaps, its most effective. But all three conferences suffered from the drawbacks notoriously incident to personal diplomacy in the Renaissance and perhaps at other periods.[70]

Other attempts at direct negotiation (inappropriately called *personal diplomacy* in English) were tried at this time, with greater or lesser success, but even the successful ones were not free of risks, as was noticed by attentive observers of international relations and by the peoples themselves. Garret Mattingly says the following about the matter:

Now and then princes were their own ambassadors, and for these occasions there were no set rules. They might be conducted with the greatest pomp or with the greatest informality. Personal interviews between the heads of states have always had obvious advantages. When they turned out well, as for instance, Lorenzo de Medici's interview with Ferrante of Naples in 1480, they gave the outcome a look of special solidity and the succesful prince an increment of that prestige so important to a Renaissance tyrant. But such interviews were risky, and politicians began to see that one of their chief risks— the fanfare of attendant publicity which advertised failure as surely as success—extended also to solemn special embassies. Inobstrusive special envoys or the still less conspicuous residents were safer.[71]

These personal meetings between monarchs happened in spite of the negative opinion of Philippe de Commynes, to which we alluded above. They were, however, isolated cases. In general, the normal system of diplomatic representation and the use of intermediaries in negotiations between sovereigns predominated at the beginning of the modern age.

The religious wars that began in Europe around 1560 shook the system of diplomatic representation, which seemed already consolidated. Around 1589, diplomatic contacts in Europe were practically interrupted except among countries of the same religious orientation. The situation was reestablished only with the peace of Westphalia in 1648, and from then on the system of diplomatic representation became stabilized and expanded all over Europe.

The importance and the extension of diplomatic activity in the modern age was signalled by a considerable bibliography appearing especially in the sixteenth and seventeenth centuries, dedicated to the exercise of the function of ambassador. Between 1498 and 1598, that is, in the span of a century, remarks Mattingly, sixteen books about diplomacy were published. In the following twenty-one years, until 1620, no less than twenty-one books about the subject were published, culminating with the publication in Seville in that year of the small treatise called *El Embajador* by the Spanish diplomat and author Juan António de Vera. This book was translated into French and published in Paris in 1642 with the title *Le Parfait Ambassadeur* and enjoyed an immense success in the seventeenth century, becoming the favorite textbook of diplomats.[72] Its fame was dethroned only by the appearance in 1716 of a treatise by the experienced French diplomat François de Callières (1645–1717), called *De la manière de négocier avec les souverains*.[73] Callière's book then became the required textbook of eighteenth-century diplomats and, even today, it still is frequently quoted. The reason for its success lies in the fact that it is written with great elegance and clarity and that it shows a profound knowledge of the subject matter. Instead of concerning himself with the superficial aspects of diplomacy or with the privileges and immunities of diplomats, Callières treats diplomatic activity proper, which he calls negotiation. His remarks on that subject are pertinent and even profound, and many of them are still entirely valid today. It can be said that, of all the authors who wrote about diplomacy before the nineteenth century, Callières was certainly the one who best comprehended the essence or the very sense of that institution.

Coming back to the negotiations that led to the signing of the treaty of Westphalia in 1648, they were not only a historical landmark inaugurating a period of great expansion of diplomatic activity, but they also introduced a new diplomatic method, so-called multilateral diplomacy. Contrary to the opinion of many authors, multilateral diplomacy was not created in the period following World War I, having already been tried in previous epochs. The innovation after World War I was the creation of a system of multilateral diplomacy with a permanent character, which was remarkably expanded after World War II.

The negotiations that led to the signing of the famous treaty of Westphalia (a set of agreements signed between October 14 and October 24, 1648) begun in 1641 in two Westphalian cities, Munster and Osnabruck. The peace between France and the Empire was negotiated at Munster and that between the

Empire and Sweden and its Protestant allies at Osnabruck. In Munster, the papal legate served as mediator, and in Osnabruck the Venetian ambassador performed the same role. The negotiations began in earnest only in 1644 and had a truly multilateral character. Portugal, which had just regained its independence, tried to be represented in the negotiations but was not allowed to because of strong opposition from Spain, and its ambassadors had to act behind the scenes.

Another important multilateral meeting in the modern age was the congress of Utrecht, which took place at the beginning of the eighteenth century and led to the agreements known as the Treaty of Utrecht, signed between January and July 1713. In this congress, which ended the War of the Spanish Succession, the representatives of France, England, the Holy Roman Empire, General States of Holland, Prussia, Savoy, Palatinate, the bishop of Munster, Trèves, Hesse, Wurtemberg, Poland, Lorraine, and Portugal participated.

CONTEMPORARY AGE

At the beginning of the contemporary age, the diplomatic institution was already fully enshrined in international law and was ruled by universal principles based on international custom and doctrine.

The democratization of public life, particularly pronounced in the nineteenth century, also led to the democratization of diplomatic personnel, which, in the modern age, was recruited mostly from the ranks of the aristocratic elite. Such a change extended considerably the recruitement base of diplomatic personnel; although this produced important consequences for the organization of the diplomatic service, it did not affect the essential role of diplomacy, namely the use of intermediaries in contacts between different centers of political power.

The greater emphasis given to juridical principles in the international domain in the contemporary age led to the establishment of the first conventional norms about the hierarchy of diplomatic agents and their respective precedence, issues that created more than a few incidents during the modern age. These norms were the result of a new multilateral congress, the Congress of Vienna, which met in 1815 in the Austrian capital to regulate the European political situation after the fall of the Napoleonic empire. The problems of rank and precedence of the various diplomatic agents was always linked to the rank of the various European states, complicating the problem and making its consequences more serious.

During the Middle Ages the pope set the order of precedence. The table or class-list of 1504, still exists. The German Emperor came first, and the Duke of Ferrara was last. The King of Portugal was sixth, the King of England seventh, and the King of Sicily was eighth. These were subject to dispute from the very first. The Spaniards, listed below the French, disputed their placement. Nicolson says, "Unseemly pushings and poutings between the French and Spanish Ambassadors" resulted, including a brawl on September 30, 1661, when the Spanish Ambassador's coach tried to push in front of the coach of the French ambassador at a procession in London. The incident led to a rupture of diplomatic relations and nearly to a war. When Russia, which had been an Asian tried to become a European power, further problems resulted. In 1768, the Russian Ambassador took the French Ambassador's place next to the Ambassador of the Emperor. The French Ambassador, who arrived late and shoved himself between the two. In the subsequent duel, the Russian Ambassador was wounded. As Nicolson says, "the whole business was becoming a farce." Worse yet, treaties were being threatened by the confusion of protocol. All the plenipotentiaries wanted to sign them first. The *alternat* was invented to deal with the problem; it provided a separate copy of each treaty or document for each plenipotentiary to sign first; this laborious method gave to each signer one copy on which his own name occupied the place of honour.

The Congress of Vienna decided wisely that the time had come to put an end to so ridiculous a system. The common-sense method was therefore adopted by which the precedence of diplomatic representatives should be governed by their actual seniority, that is by the date of the official notification of their arrival at the seat of their mission. The Vienna Règlement, in spite of Castlereagh's scepticism, did in fact settle the precedence problem for more than a hundred years. It may well be that some future Congress will find itself obliged, in view of the multiplicity of Embassies which have since been created, to adopt a further Règlement under which Ambassadors are classified as of the first, second or third category. This, it is to be expected, will provoke a most invidious discussion.[74]

Nicolson's concluding comment about a future ranking of ambassadors by categories arises out of the typical ironical vein of the author. Nicolson wrote this passage in 1945; the United Nations had already enshrined the principle of absolute equality not only of the nations but also of their representatives, one that was already implicit in the decisions of the Congress of Vienna. Although the principle of equality may seem absurd in many of its practical applications, we do not believe it will be easily changed.

As a note to Nicolson's words, we should remark that the system of setting the precedence of ambassadors according to the date of the beginning of their missions was introduced by the Marquis of Pombal, the Portuguese prime minister. In 1760, on the occasion of the marriage of the princess of Brazil, Pombal announced, in a circular sent to all the diplomatic representations in Lisbon, that, on this occasion, the embassies to the Portuguese court, with the exception of the nuncio and the Emperor's ambassador, should order their visits or obtain appointments according to the date of their credentials. The French foreign minister at the time, Choiseul, declared when the matter was submitted to him that France would not accept the new rule in any case and did not recognize any right on the part of the Portuguese monarch to establish new rules in this matter. Spain reacted in the same way, and Vienna, whose position was not affected, told the French government that it would support it in opposing the ridiculous pretension of the Portuguese minister.[75] The "ridiculous pretension of the Portuguese minister" came, however, to be adopted by the Congress of Vienna, which met, ironically, in the Austrian capital, and even the representative of the Emperor of Austria had, from then on, to submit to the general rule, from which only the nuncio was excepted in Catholic countries.

The agreement signed in Vienna on March 19, 1815, regulated only the problem of rank and precedence among diplomatic agents. Many other aspects of diplomatic activity continued to be regulated only by custom and doctrine, with all the variation allowed by the absence of conventional norms. Several attempts were made to codify the norms applicable to diplomatic activity. The League of Nations, through its Commission of Experts for the Codification of International Law, tried to make some progress in this area by presenting reports about diplomatic prerogatives and immunities and the classification of diplomatic agents. However, the work of this commission had no practical follow-up.

The Sixth American International Conference, meeting in Havana in 1928, produced the "Convention about Diplomatic Officials," concluded on February 28 of that year and dealing fundamentally with the rights and duties of diplomatic agents. This convention, however, was to be applied only with a very narrow scope and, as a consequence, it was eventually forgotten.

The United Nations, through its International Law Commission, also dealt with the problems relative to the exercise of diplomatic activity and by General Assembly Resolution 1450 (CXIV), adopted on December 7, 1960, it called a United Nations Conference about Diplomatic Relations and Immunities that took place in Vienna between March 2 and April 14, 1961. This conference produced the "Vienna Convention on Diplomatic Relations," of April 18, 1961, which entered into force in 1964. It has been signed by most states and presently is the fundamental instrument that regulates diplomatic relations. The convention was completed by the "Vienna Convention on Consular Relations," concluded on April 24, 1963, and by the "Vienna Convention about State Representation in Relations with International Organizations of a Universal Character" of March 14, 1975.[76]

Another important transformation of diplomacy in the contemporary age was the institutionalization of multilateral diplomacy with the creation, since the nineteenth century, of international organizations of various types. As a result of the Treaty of Paris of 1814 and of the Congress of Vienna of 1815, the International Commission of the Rhine was created. The

Treaty of Paris that ended the Crimean War established the International Commission of the Danube in 1856. Both organizations were of a permanent character, several states being represented in them. The Universal Telegraphic Union was also created in 1856, becoming later the International Telecommunications Union. In 1874 the Universal Postal Union appeared. Many other so-called administrative unions were created during the nineteenth century and at the beginning of the twentieth century, up to the start of World War I in 1914. All these organizations were permanent and multilateral in character but had limited powers dealing with a precise and specialized sector of interstate interests.

In 1919, as a result of the peace conference that ended the 1914 war, the League of Nations was created. The League was the first universal organization of a permanent and multilateral character, and its central goal was to guarantee peace among states. It was thus the highest expression of multilateral diplomacy.

The peace conference that met at Versailles in 1919 was strongly influenced by the thinking of President Woodrow Wilson, who on January 8, 1918, had proclaimed his famous "fourteen points," one of which proposed the creation of the League of Nations. Wilson personally led the American delegation to the negotiations. The first of the "Fourteen Points" demanded that, in the future, there should be agreements negotiated openly and no secret understandings between countries.[77] Harold Nicolson said that the Treaty of Versailles, though it was an open covenant, because its terms were openly published "was not 'openly arrived at.' "[78] Nicolson does not dispute, naturally, the need for secrecy in these negotiations; he merely stresses the fact that Wilson's "open negotiations" are a practical impossibility and that the American President stood on very shaky ground by failing to understand the enormous difference between "open agreements" and "open negotiations," that is, between politics and negotiation. An American diplomat, Charles W. Thayer, remarks about this:

Much of the failure of the Versailles venture was due to American misunderstandings of the function of diplomacy. Despite his intellectual equipment and academic training, Wilson, like most of his compatriots, clung to the myth that Machiavellian diplomacy had been responsible for the war. Mistaking diplomacy for policy-making, he put the blame not on the policies and their creators but on the men who had to carry them out. He was determined therefore that the post-war world was to be made safe for democracy by making it free of the "old diplomacy."[79]

Wilson's attempts to create a new diplomatic era, that of *democratic diplomacy*, contributed only to provoking a deplorable confusion between diplomacy and foreign policy, between political action and its instrument. This confusion, as we already saw, continues to our day to mar American political works and others influenced by them.

This was not however the only consequence of the failed intervention of the American president in the peace negotiations. The League of Nations, in which so many postwar men placed so much hope as a guarantor of world peace, also failed. The American Congress did not ratify the agreement that created the League, depriving it of its most important associate and discrediting the president who had been its great inspirer. Russia, in the grips of a revolution of gigantic proportions, also did not participate in the organization from the beginning, being admitted only in 1934. By then, Germany and Japan had already left it, in 1933. Italy withdrew in 1937. During its twenty years' existence, several serious acts of international aggression took place without any efficient intervention of the League of Nations. The last such aggression, Germany's invasion of Poland in 1939, was the *coup de grâce* to an already moribund organization.

Some specialized agencies created under the aegis of the League of Nations survived its disappearance. The International Labor Organization, founded in 1919 and one of the most felicitous creations of the League, is one of them.

During the last world war, the bases were established for a new international organization of a universal character, the United Nations, which, with its numerous specialized agencies, constitutes a complex system of international institutions through which multilateral diplomacy reached its zenith.

The project for the creation of a world political organization was launched in the Dumbarton Oaks Conference, meeting between August 21 and October 7, 1944, with representatives of the United States, Great Britain, Soviet Union, and China. In that conference, a document was prepared that served as the basis for the San Francisco Conference, called by those powers and begun on April 25, 1945. After two months of negotiations, the United Nations Charter was signed on June 26 of that year.

The United Nations and its specialized agencies and the regional organizations created in the post-war era—such as the North Atlantic Treaty Organization, Organization for Economic Cooperation and Development, Organization of American States, Central Treaty Organization, South East Asia Treaty Organization, Australia-New Zealand-United States Treaty, Organization for African Unity, European Economic Community, European Free Trade Area, Western European Union, European Council, and Comecon, to mention but a few—gave multilateral diplomacy an unprecedented importance. Later on, we will examine more closely the fundamental characteristics of this type of diplomacy, which can be considered one of the creations of our age.

A less fortunate product of the postwar periods (of World Wars I and II) was the huge increase in the use of direct negotiation, to the detriment of diplomatic negotiation. In this matter, Anglo-Saxon terminology also adopted an unfortunate term to designate the phenomenon. English language authors usually call this type of negotiation, carried out directly between statesmen, *personal diplomacy*, which, on reflection, is an absurd expression. In French writings, we sometimes find the expression *direct negotiation*, which seems to us more appropriate and much clearer, since it describes a negotiation between two holders of political power without the intervention of intermediaries.[80]

President Wilson's influence in this matter was also decisive because of his decision not only to be present at the Versailles negotiations but to personally lead the American delegation. The president acted thus against the opinion of his most experienced advisers and, in fact, the consequences of his action were far from positive.

In spite of the warnings of Philippe de Commynes and so many others, of which we find a recent echo in Dean Acheson's writings, statesmen all over the world tend to meet with each other more and more often and to engage in direct negotiations, which often are not even prepared by the competent intermediaries. This trend accelerated considerably after the end of World War II because of the remarkable increase in the availability of logistical means, namely the telephone and the airplane, which made frequent contacts between statesmen possible, no matter how far from each other their countries might be.

We shall have occasion further ahead to say a few words about the consequences of this new trend and about the effects it has produced on the diplomatic institution.

SYNTHESIS

The social sciences cannot produce on demand the facts on which their theories are based. They substantially differ from the physical sciences in this respect. But, by the study of history, they can investigate the genesis and the evolution of the facts of greater interest to them. Thus we can say that history is the experimental lab of the social sciences.

The brief study we made of the diplomatic institution—although not as extended and in depth as we would wish—allows us nevertheless to extract a few conclusions of some importance for the elaboration of the concept and general theory of diplomacy.

The conclusions are the following:

a) The use of intermediaries between holders of political power of two nations or different political units has always existed, at least since the time when societies acquired a political organization and felt the need to establish contact.

b) In all civilizations of antiquity, intermediaries or diplomats were used in relations between different peoples.

c) The diplomatic institution was an important and constant element of the organization of the State in Greek and Roman civilization.

d) In the Middle Ages, although monarchs sometimes arranged meetings and even direct negotiations, negotiations through intermediaries predominated.

e) Some direct negotiations tried at the beginning of the modern age were a complete failure, and those rare ones that succeeded did so at great risks.

f) Developing a trend arising in the Middle Ages, the modern age enshrined the principle of permanent diplomatic representations, which constitute an acknowledgement by the different states that diplomacy is indispensable.

g) In the modern age, the system of multilateral diplomacy was also enshrined but still with an episodic character, to solve important problems of interest for a group of countries.

h) At the beginning of the contemporary age, the first conventional rules defining the rank and precedence of diplomatic agents were established. These conventional rules were amplified to other aspects of diplomatic activity, and a true international statute of the diplomatic agent was created in the Vienna Conference about diplomatic relations of 1961.

i) Multilateral diplomacy was also institutionalized during the contemporary age with the creation of several international organizations of regional or universal character, thus establishing a vast system of multilateral diplomacy no less important than the traditional system of bilateral diplomacy.

j) Still in the contemporary age, direct contacts between holders of political power were much increased due to the extraordinary progress of means of communication. These contacts often took the form of direct negotiation, with or without previous diplomatic preparation.

k) The continuity of the diplomatic institution throughout thousands of years and in all known civilizations shows that diplomacy is an institution inherent to international life itself, one that may undergo transformations or may be used with more or less intensity, but cannot be dispensed with.

Chapter 2

THE PURE CONCEPT OF DIPLOMACY

DIFFERENT DEFINITIONS OF DIPLOMACY; THEIR ANALYSIS

The most reputed dictionaries and encyclopedias and all the authors who, in one way or another, have treated the subject of diplomacy have given an enormous number of definitions of the term. As a rule, these definitions are imprecise, incomplete, or clearly erroneous. It would be useless and superfluous to list here all or most of them. We can, however, place them in four groups in order to examine what is deficient or improper in them.

We shall mention first the definitions that equate diplomacy with foreign policy. In the introduction, we already took the opportunity to allude to this improper identification and to note how widespread it is, even among authors specializing in the theory of international relations and career diplomats. Our comments about this problem seem sufficient, and therefore we will not say much more about it.[1] As a reminder, let us just recall that Hans J. Morgenthau conceives diplomacy as "the formation and execution of foreign policy."[2] The insistence with which political scientists use the term *diplomacy* to mean foreign policy may be said to be almost an addiction and, in certain respects, it is a bizarre phenomenon. Professors of political theory have a well-known propensity to treat diplomats with haughtiness and even scorn and yet, when they speak about foreign policy, they almost always prefer to call it *diplomacy*.

Second, we will refer to the definitions that equate diplomacy with the instrument or technique of foreign policy. The definition given by Jacques Chazelle is among these, when he says: "The term diplomacy means . . . the set of means and specific activities used by a State to serve its foreign policy."[3] Chazelle judiciously adds that this definition is wider than the definition of diplomacy as "the art of negotiation" and excludes "the common but abusive identification of diplomacy with foreign policy as such, of which diplomacy is only an instrument."[4] The Soviet *Diplomatic Dictionary*, published in Moscow between 1948 and 1950, also defines *diplomacy* as "the technical instrument for the implementation of foreign policy."[5] Along the same lines, professor K. J. Holsti says in his textbook on international politics that "most official attempts to wield influence abroad are carried out through formal diplomatic channels or by direct communication between foreign ministers and heads of state." And he adds: "The function of the diplomat is not so much to formulate his government's goals as to explain them abroad."[6] And this author, distinguishing diplomacy from direct contacts between holders of political power treats the former under the general category of "policy instruments."

These definitions are only partially correct. While it is true that diplomacy is an instrument of foreign policy, it is equally true that it is not the only one. As we have seen, others also exist.

Third, we will mention the definitions identifying diplomacy with international negotiation. When Callières mentions diplomatic activity, he identifies it with negotiation, although it must be said that this author uses the word negotiation in a very wide sense. Charles de Martens, author of a famous *Guide Diplomatique*, first published in 1822, in later editions defines diplomacy as "the science or art of negotiation."[7] The *Oxford English Dictionary* defines diplomacy as "the conduct of international relations by negotiation." Satow, author of a popular diplomatic guide, defines it as "the conduct of business between States by peaceful means,"[8] which is equivalent to the preceding definitions.

Many other examples could be given of definitions identifying diplomacy with negotiation. Although they contain much that is true, these definitions are imprecise or incomplete. In effect, although negotiation, taken in its narrower sense of preparing, discussing and concluding an agreement between two states, is the most important part of diplomatic activity, it does not encompass all of it. Collecting and transmiting to his government information about the different aspects of the life of the country where the diplomat is posted are activities that cannot be called negotiation. The same happens with other aspects of diplomatic activity, as we shall see more clearly later on.

It must be said, however, that Callières's concept of negotiation is so wide that it encompasses pratically all diplomatic activity.

Callières, in effect, identifies the diplomat (a term that, by the way, he never uses) with the negotiator and in his small treatise *De la manière de négocier avec les Souverains*, the terms negotiator, ambassador, or envoy are used indifferently to designate the same function. When describing "the functions of the negotiator," Callières says, for example: "The functions of a minister sent to a foreign country are chiefly two: one is to care for the interests of his Sovereign in that country and the other is to discover the interests of others."[9] And after this definition of the functions of a diplomatic agent, Callières goes on to describe his day-to-day activities.

Therefore, were we to adopt a definition of diplomacy as wide as Callières's, we could accept the term negotiation to describe diplomatic activity. However, we would still be unable to identify diplomacy with negotiation since some negotiations, which we call direct negotiations, take place without the intervention of intermediaries or diplomatic agents.

Fourth and last, we will briefly mention the definitions describing diplomacy as the activity of diplomats. These are, of course, tautological definitions, of the type "medicine is the art practiced by doctors," which, although correct, do not tell us anything about the nature of the activity they pretend to define. Thus, the *Oxford English Dictionary*, besides the already quoted definition of diplomacy as negotiation, also defines it as "the business or art of the diplomatist." Morton Kaplan says that diplomacy is "the execution by the diplomats of the strategy aiming at the realization of national interests in the international field."[10]

Such definitions, although they tell us nothing of the essence of diplomacy, at least have the virtue of being exact. In truth, no one can deny that diplomacy is the business of diplomats or that medicine is the activity practiced by doctors and so on.

ESSENTIAL ELEMENTS OF THE CONCEPT OF DIPLOMACY

All of the several types of definition just mentioned have some elements of truth, with the exception of the first, which equates diplomacy with foreign policy. The latter type of definition arises out of a deplorable conceptual confusion to which we already referred more than once and that has beleaguered the literature on the theory and history of international relations and foreign policy. If we eliminate this confusion once and for all, we can say with certainty that diplomacy is one instrument of foreign policy among others; it is also a fact that diplomacy is negotiation between two or more states, if the term negotiation is understood in its widest sense, and if taken in a narrow sense, that negotiation is the most important part of diplomatic activity; and lastly, it is also a fact—so obvious it is a truth of La Palisse—that diplomacy is the activity of diplomats. By combining these different elements, we will perhaps be able to find a precise definition of what diplomacy, in essence, is.

Whether it is considered from the point of view of political theory, history, or international law, diplomacy, like war, is, in effect, an instrument of foreign policy. Disregarding this fundamental fact has provoked considerable theoretical confusion, with unfortunate practical consequences. The fact that certain diplomats may be able to influence the formulation of a given foreign policy or that they may ascend to the posts of head of government or minister for foreign affairs doubtlessly has also contributed to maintain the common confusion between foreign policy and diplomacy. However, when a diplomat influences the formulation of a given foreign policy, he is not acting as a diplomat, because he is either contributing to the creation of foreign policy or he is simply expressing his political opinions as a citizen who is entitled to do so. The fact that diplomacy as a whole, with its particular experience in the field of foreign relations, may influence the formulation of a given foreign policy does not mean that, in itself, it is any less an instrument. Although the Marquis of Pombal, Prince Metternich, and Prince Otto von Bismarck were career diplomats, this does not mean they should be called diplomats when holding political office, or, for that matter, that any member of a government should be called a diplomat. While he is part of the government, a foreign minister acts as a politician and not as a diplomat, even if he is a career diplomat. A diplomat is an intermediary between two governments, something a minister cannot be since he belongs to one of these governments.

Diplomacy is also an instrument to put the governments of two or more states in contact with each other. In this sense it is said that diplomacy is the art of negotiation, if the word is taken in its widest sense. In order to avoid further conceptual confusion in a field where it is already rife, we prefer to keep the term *negotiation* to signify the preparation, discussion and conclusion of an agreement between two governments and use the general term *contact* to signify all types of communication and dialogue between two different political units. This contact must be essentially peaceful in nature, since those of a violent nature fall outside the scope of diplomacy. The goal of diplomacy is precisely to try to solve by nonviolent means all problems that may arise between two states. We will say therefore that diplomacy is an instrument of foreign policy to establish peaceful contacts between the holders of political power of two states.

This pre-definition comes close to reality but it still lacks the essential element, that is, the intervention of the intermediary to establish this contact, since it can also be established directly by the holders of political power of two states. The intervention of the intermediary in the establishment of this contact does not arise merely out of convenience, tradition, or other reasons having to do with the interests of a class of civil servants. It is an essential requirement of the system, which, from the most remote times of the history of humanity, has been intuitively perceived by holders of political power of independent political units. The study of direct meetings between holders of political power of different states and, especially, the attempts at direct negotiation between them sharply highlight the essential character of the use of intermediaries. One aspect that historians particularly stress about these direct meetings is the risk that the holders of political power may fall under the control of the other party. It is curious to notice the precautions taken by Caesar when he decided to meet the German king Ariovistus. The precautions taken by each of them practically eliminated all possibility of a successful negotiation, which would have been possible only in an atmosphere of mutual trust.[11] Naturally, those risks were greater and more frequent in the most remote times of our history, but they were not entirely absent in meetings taking place in the modern age. The initiative taken by Lorenzo the Magnificent to negotiate directly with King Ferrante of Naples, although successful, met with reservations, because he put Florence at grave risk by placing himself at the mercy of a rival foreign sovereign.[12] In the contemporary age, Napoleon, following the ancient and prudent monarchical method of meeting in the middle of a bridge, had a conference with emperor Alexander I in a boat anchored in the middle of the Memel River. It can be said that these risks no longer exist in our time, which is at least partially correct. But for many centuries, they were real, and the use of intermediaries in contacts between states or different political units was a necessity that gave strong and deep roots to the diplomatic institution.

Even if these risks could be neglected, the most discerning observers have always considered meetings between monarchs or political leaders of different states to be inconvenient.

Philippe de Commynes wrote some famous pages condemning them, in which he says that, as a rule, they produced more enmities than friendships among monarchs. Large parties participated in the meetings, and they tended to exaggerate and amplify small faults committed by both sides, to the point of influencing the respective sovereigns or the important persons that accompanied them.[13] A more up-to-date testimony about this matter is given by Dean Acheson, who, in his memoirs, openly condemns summit conferences or state visits for producing weak results and sometimes worsening relations between states.[14]

However, let us look at this matter more closely and examine in greater depth the fundamental reasons that justify the permanent use of intermediaries between the holders of political power of the different states.

In the first place, direct meetings between political leaders of different states often produce a mutual dislike, or on the contrary, special ties of friendship between them. Neither dislikes nor even ties of friendship favor the objective defense of national interests. Those who are responsible for formulating and conducting a country's foreign policy must be free of any subjective influences in the appreciation of the relations of their country with another.

In the second place, meetings between political leaders of two states, especially when they have one or several precise objectives, create expectations among the two peoples that often are not met, resulting in domestic political problems.

In the third place, political leaders are usually received by their hosts with great honors and consideration, sometimes constraining them, for fear of offending their hosts, to make decisions that they would not have made if they were acting more freely.

But, in the fourth place, and most important, a negotiation always requires mutual concessions, adjustments, and compromises and is almost always characterized by advances and setbacks, moments of crisis and breaking points—things to which, by the very nature of his functions, a political leader cannot submit. A political leader, be it a head of state or a head of government or a minister of a government, represents a sovereign organ and cannot easily submit to the rules of the game of a negotiation, because he is invested with sovereign functions that do not allow him to make concessions to the representatives of another power that could be interpreted as weakness. Such concessions are necessary for progress to be made in a negotiation and to conclude it sucessfully; when they are made by an intermediary, a diplomatic representative, their import is not as great as when they are made by a holder of political power. A diplomatic agent can always be contradicted from above or even substituted without difficulty or inconvenience, whereas the same cannot happen with a political leader. Dean Acheson stresses this aspect with rare pertinence when he says the following about direct negotiations between political leaders: "When a chief of state or head of government makes a fumble, the goal line is open behind him. This I was first to learn in my first experience with this dangerous diplomatic method, which has much attraction for American presidents." And Dean Rusk, another American Secretary of State, remarked about the same matter: "The direct confrontation of the chiefs of government of the great powers involve an extra tension because the court of last resort is in session."[15]

In the fifth place, we will mention another important reason added by George Kennan:

When persons of supreme or high authority deal directly with one another, there is a tendency for their governments to take on a personal quality and to depend for their validity, to some extent, on the personal relationship that has been established. This is sometimes fine as long as it lasts; but the agreement is then largely vitiated if one or the other of them falls from office. Agreements concluded through the regular diplomatic channels, time-consuming and cumbersome as they may be, and thus regarded as agreements between governments rather than between individuals tend to be more carefully worked out, less personally conditioned, and more enduring.[16]

Finally, when for whatever circumstance the negotiations become embittered, as often happens, the direct confrontation of statesmen inevitably creates risks of international tension, whereas the same is not necessarily true if the negotiations are conducted by intermediaries. Recall what happened in the famous meeting between President Dwight D. Eisenhower and Nikita Khruschev, in Paris on May 1960. The Soviet political leader made violent accusations to the American President about the U2 plane that had been shot down by Soviet air defenses, with the result that the meeting was a complete failure. If Eisenhower had not been a military hero, and therefore a man who could not be suspected of lack of military courage, and who enjoyed great prestige in his own country, the incident could have had grave consequences not only for the two superpowers but also for all humanity.

The truth, by the way, is that the profound, although not readily admitted, reason for most meetings between political chiefs of different states lies in purely domestic considerations and not in foreign policy requirements. The latter generally do not require such meetings, as a statesman of integrity and experience like Dean Acheson courageously confesses.

We must however except from this negative appreciation the meetings of statesmen within the framework of certain international organizations, especially military alliances or those whose aim is the political integration of a group of states. In these special cases, the meetings are carefully prepared by the respective secretariats and permanent missions whose fundamental task is to conclude the negotiation in course and to constantly give support to meetings at the political level. The usefulness of this kind of meeting is manifest, not only as way of giving a political backing and impulse to those organizations, but also, in very special instances, to solve certain residual questions of eminently political character that can only be addressed at high level. Bilateral meetings at a high level or even those of a multilateral ad hoc character could be more fruitful if they took place in identical cirumstances, which unfortunately is not the case. Nonetheless, certain drawbacks that were already pointed out would not be eliminated.

Everything we have already said about this matter was meant to underline the need to use intermediaries in contacts between states, and the last remarks we made only confirm this need. If we now examine the etymology of the word *diplo-*

macy, we see that it comes from *diplomat* and in this connection the definition of diplomacy as the activity of diplomats is also correct. Diplomat comes, on the other hand, from the Greek word *diplôma* (*dipló* = folded in two + suffix *ma* = object). In the Roman and Byzantine epochs the word diploma meant a permission to use public transportation, a kind of passport.[17] Later, however, the word came to be used to designate all solemn documents issued by official chancelleries, particularly those setting down agreements between sovereigns and so the officials whose business it was to elaborate these documents were called diplomats. In 1693, Gottfried Leibniz published in Hanover, a *Codex Juris Gentium Diplomaticus* containing documents relating to international relations, thus attributing to the adjective *diplomatic* the meaning of something related to international relations. Leibniz's example was followed by Baron Jean C. de Dumont, who in 1725 began to publish in Paris the famous *Corps Universel Diplomatique du Droit des Gens*. According to the German historian Otto Ranke, toward the middle of the eighteenth century, the expression *diplomatic corps* began to be used in Vienna to designate the group of personnel serving in the foreign missions.[18] Around 1787, the *Annual Register*, published in London, used the adjective *diplomatic* about the personnel serving in missions abroad.[19] Thus, it is not surprising that Edmund Burke, writing in 1796, used the expression *diplomacy* to designate the group of chiefs of mission accredited to Paris.[20] However, it seems that in 1791 the word *diplomacy* was already used in France to designate the activity of diplomats.[21]

The word *diplomacy*, therefore, has not been part of political vocabulary for very long, but there is no doubt it first appeared to designate the activity of diplomats, that is of those officials whose business was foreign relations. Thus, the etymological meaning of the word coincides with the material meaning that we have already given, one of whose elements is the use of intermediaries in contacts between different political powers.

However, to complete the definition of diplomacy we have been constructing, it is necessary to add one last element. A state that wants to carry out a friendly policy vis-à-vis another state sends to it a representative with the mandate of promoting good relations between them. But if this envoy is not recognized by the receiving state as a legitimate representative of the sending state, he will not be able to carry out his mission for want of that initial official contact indispensable to start a dialogue between these states. Recognition of the representativeness of the intermediaries is therefore an essential element of the diplomatic institution and not simply a formality. Similarly, the inviolability of the duly accredited intermediaries is not a privilege, as it is sometimes wrongly asserted, but an essential characteristic deriving from the very nature of the diplomatic institution, because without this reciprocal inviolability, the institution could not exist. Thus, it is not surprising to hear Caesar assert vigorously that the inviolability of ambassadors is something sacred and acknowledged as such by all civilized peoples.[22]

THE PURE CONCEPT OF DIPLOMACY

This last element completes the analysis of the concept of diplomacy which, according to us, can be defined as follows:

a) an instrument of foreign policy

b) for the establishment and development of peaceful contacts between the governments of different states

c) through the use of intermediaries

d) mutually recognized by the respective parties.

These intermediaries are called *diplomatic agents*.

Diplomacy thus understood is called by us *pure diplomacy* to distinguish it from all other senses in which the word diplomacy is frequently used, some of which include elements that have nothing to do with diplomatic activity, while others lack one or more of the essential elements of the definition given above. A pure theory of diplomacy that allow us to understand this old institution in its exact form and perspective can be built only on the foundation of a precise concept of this kind. In the state of conceptual confusion in which the theory and history of foreign policy find themselves, the formulation of such a pure theory seems to us to be required in order to clarify ideas and avoid mistaken notions that have generated a number of practical negative consequences. It will suffice to take a look at the vast modern bibliography about the theory of international relations and foreign policy, its history and the applicable public law, to see the utility of such a pure theory. The goal of the present study is precisely to try to isolate conceptually, through the application of a pure concept of diplomacy, what belongs to diplomacy as a pure instrument of foreign policy, eliminating from its study the elements that do not belong to it and serve only to confuse concepts. It may be a doomed enterprise if we think that not much progress has been made in separating the two in political literature, since Harold Nicolson vehemently protested against the confusion between diplomacy and foreign policy in 1939, in the first edition of his essay *Diplomacy*. The confusion is rife especially in American academic literature, which is certainly the most developed in the field of the theory of international relations.

The concept of pure diplomacy naturally implies the idea of a pure diplomat, that is, an official who acts solely as the instrument of a given foreign policy. In reality, however, diplomats can also have political functions. In effect, given their experience and familiarity with the field of foreign policy, at times diplomats are called upon to perform political functions, or, especially when they are posted to headquarters, to perform the role of political advisers to the minister for foreign affairs or to the government as a whole. This fact, however, should not lead to any deviation from the pure concept of diplomacy, which must be understood as an autonomous category and the only valid foundation for a scientific theory of diplomacy. The diplomatic agent as such acts exclusively within the scope of diplomacy, and he or she should not forget it. When he intervenes in the formulation of a given foreign policy, he is not acting as a diplomat but as a politician or political adviser. The two functions can be confused in practice but, theoretically, they are wholly distinct.

It is appropriate to recall at this moment something we

pointed out earlier, namely that Harold Nicolson, after pro-
testing against the widespread confusion between the concepts of foreign policy and diplomacy, confuses them himself.
Nicolson tried to justify himself by saying: "The theory of policy and the theory of negotiation are interactive."[23] If this
statement seems to us factually true, the premise of Nicolson's argument, however, is wrong. Theory is one thing and
practice another. In practice, a diplomatic agent can, in fact,
simultaneously exercise the functions of a political agent, and
we can say that the two activities interpenetrate. However,
the theory of foreign policy is one thing and the theory of diplomacy another, and there cannot be, in the purely theoretical field, interpenetration and confusion between them, because they are, by definition, autonomous theories, no matter
how close the links between the political and diplomatic activities of a given agent.

We must add that Nicolson left us some important observations about diplomatic activity that are valid contributions
for building a diplomatic theory. But his theoretical weakness
is quite patent in all his works about diplomacy. This example
demonstrates once more the need to build a pure theory of
diplomacy, in order to avoid the confusions that affect even
the best documented and most experienced scholars of diplomacy.

Chapter 3

DIPLOMATIC MORPHOLOGY

OLD AND NEW DIPLOMACY

Works about the theory and history of foreign relations and even diplomatic guides frequently refer to two supposedly contrasting types or forms of diplomacy: the old diplomacy and the new diplomacy. In our opinion, this is a superficial distinction, arising once again out of conceptual mistakes already pointed out. In general, the following characteristics are attributed to the old diplomacy: to consider Europe to be the center of gravity of international politics; that the so-called great powers have the chief responsibility for the conduct of international politics; believing that the diplomatic service in all countries has common and identical standards of professional conduct; to consider negotiation to be not an isolated episode, but an ongoing process that must always be confidential in its diverse steps. By contrast, the new diplomacy is supposed to have the following characteristics: to consider that the composition of international society has changed radically and that the center of gravity of international politics has been gradually deviating from Europe; that diplomatic traditions have been altered by cultural diversity and ideological differences; that the progress of the means of communication and the impact of public opinion have considerably increased international conflicts and tensions; that there are alternative methods of international contact through the direct communication between political leaders and foreign ministers and through the activities of multilateral organs and institutions (such as international organizations and conferences). These characteristics are mentioned by a diplomat and student of diplomatic technique, Harold Nicolson, and by an expert in the theory of international relations, Professor Joseph Frankel.[1]

Regarding this distinction between new and old diplomacy, we will begin by quoting—as many already have—the words of Jules Cambon who, in 1926, wrote:

New diplomacy, old diplomacy are words that correspond to nothing real. What tends to change is the exterior, the attire of diplomacy, if you will. But the substance will always be the same because human nature does not change, nations will continue to have but one way to solve their differences, and the word of a honest man will always be the best tool available to a Government to defend its points of view.[2]

These are the words of a highly intelligent man, who was deeply knowledgeable about diplomatic activity. As we shall discover later, they hold a lot of truth. What is most surprising is that Harold Nicolson quotes Cambon's words after listing the characteristics we mentioned as defining the old diplomacy. Furthermore, Nicolson, who vehemently criticized the frequent confusion between diplomacy and foreign policy, includes among these characteristics some that clearly belong to foreign policy and have nothing to do with diplomacy.

In fact, considering Europe to be the center of gravity of international politics or the great powers to be the main actors in international politics are characteristics of a given foreign policy and not of diplomacy, which is an instrument of foreign policy. Some of the characteristics of the new diplomacy mentioned above, such as the deviation from Europe of the center of gravitation of international politics or the pressures arising out of the progress of communications and the impact of public opinion, belong to the same class.

As for the other characteristics that were mentioned, such as the uniform standards of the diplomatic service or the confidentiality of negotiations, it is not clear how they serve to contrast or distinguish between the so-called old and new diplomacy. The former characteristic really is a secondary or, to use Cambon's word, exterior element; the latter, that is the confidentiality of negotiations is an essential element of the negotiating process which can be more or less important and include certain aspects but not others but cannot in any case serve to contrast the old and the new diplomacy, since the problems it generates are the same at all times. This is true, of course, as long as we do not commit the old mistake of confusing negotiation and diplomacy with foreign policy. In effect, some authors identify the old diplomacy with secret diplomacy and the new diplomacy with open diplomacy. This is evidently a conceptual confusion, to which we will refer in greater detail further ahead.

With regard to the new means of communication and the impact of public opinion in the political life of states, they have no doubt exerted in recent times an important influence on the making of foreign policy. They have even led states, at times, to do without the diplomatic instrument, using others instead, but they did not fundamentally alter the nature of diplomacy in its exact sense. Diplomacy, like any other state activity, has now more efficient and rapid work tools available; however, this fact has not changed its essence, and it is a grave mistake to suppose that these new and better tools benefitted certain state sectors but not diplomacy.

As for multilateral diplomacy, as we also shall see more clearly later on, it cannot be said to be a characteristic of modern diplomacy, and much less can the two be identified.[3] The multilateral type of diplomacy is much older and its use in past times was more frequent than may be thought; on the other hand the interpenetration between multilateral and bilateral diplomacy in our own times is much greater than is sometimes believed.

What we can say by way of conclusion is that, throughout history, the tasks and the style of diplomacy have changed considerably, but that diplomacy itself, as an instrument of foreign policy, has always kept its defining traits: the use of intermediaries in relations between the holders of political power of different states. Obviously, the diplomats of antiquity, of the Middle Ages, or of the eighteenth century did not act in the same manner, nor were their functions as complex as those of the diplomat of today. This is the result of the change in social habits and lifestyle from past to present times, on the one hand, and, on the other, of the greater complexity in the relations existing today between modern states.

Before the democratization of political life, diplomats represented their respective countries in diverse, more or less autocratic courts, but, in all cases, etiquette was considered a fundamental element in ruling circles, even if its rules were not equally rigorous from place to place. Strict obedience to the rules of etiquette was an important element to determine the greater or lesser success of a diplomatic agent. The requirements of protocol changed with the progressive democratization of public life, but that does not mean that protocol no longer has an important function in public life. Although these requirements may seem superfluous or even ridiculous to some, they perform an essential role, not only in international contacts, in which protocol is a way of defending the fundamental principle of equality between states, but also in the domestic political life of all countries. Experience tells us that those who openly proclaim their contempt for protocol rules and even laugh at them are often the first to complain if, in a given public act, they are not seated where they think they are entitled to be or if they are not treated with the amount of deference that they believe is deserved by their social or official position.

Although, as we already said, rules of protocol decreased enormously in number in modern times, some people still think of diplomats as creatures fundamentally and indeed excessively concerned with protocol and little else. This idea is, of course, totally wrong in the great majority of cases. In fact, most rules of social intercourse to which diplomats submit, or submitted in bygone days, are not and were not exclusive to diplomats, but rather were social habits and norms followed in the social or official circles where diplomats generally practice or practiced their professional activity. As for official protocol, it is not established by a given country's diplomatic corps but by its official authorities. Lastly, we should note that not all diplomatic agents of a given diplomatic service deal with every aspect of diplomatic activity; however, it is those in charge of state protocol who most frequently contact political leaders and the great figures of a country's political and social life and, through the media, the public, with the result that these personalities and the public itself associate the image of a diplomat to that of an agent of protocol. It is not surprising to find this simplistic and even ridiculous idea in the minds of badly informed people, but it is shocking to see it shared by persons of the highest intellectual level, some of whom do not even shy away from expressing it in writing.

The other important aspect we wish to focus upon concerning this matter of old and new diplomacy is the fact that, in the past, relations among states in general had little content, and the functions of diplomatic agents were limited to those of representing their respective countries and informing them, and occasionally to negotiating a specific matter (a political alliance, a commercial treaty, a royal marriage, etc.). On the contrary, relations among modern states are extremely complex and varied, which, by itself, gives modern diplomacy a richer and more diversified content, requiring better trained diplomatic agents. It is enough to mention the field of communications to have an idea about the multiplicity of links connecting the different states, even those that are geographically distant from each other. Telecommunications, postal and aerial communications, navigation links, railways, roads, and so on—these are fields in which states must cooperate. Some of these fields did not exist in the past, and in others there was little cooperation and sometimes none at all. It is evident that relations among states include many other and highly varied fields, such as health, cultural exchanges, financial and economic cooperation, emigration, scientific and technical cooperation, sports, and the protection of trademarks and intellectual property. Not to mention, of course, relations of an essentially political character, which are more or less intense according to the participation of the concerned states in political groupings, their geographical proximity, and their ideological affinities.

Thus, we can say, to set straight those who are still attached to the tired and illusory distinction between old and new diplomacy, that today diplomatic etiquette is reduced to a minimum and that the content of international relations has known an extraordinary development. The old diplomacy, then, had less content, while paying more attention to protocol, and the new diplomacy devotes less attention to protocol, while possessing a greater and more varied content. However, this change is the result not of an essential difference between the old and the new diplomacy but rather of the change of social habits on the one hand, and on the other, of the development of interstate relations due to the progress of humanity.

By the way, this progress afforded diplomacy highly sophisticated technologies that were not available to the diplomats of the past. The documents produced by the diplomats of today, for example, are typewritten, photocopied, or microfilmed and not just handwritten as was the case with diplomatic documents of the eighteenth and most of the nineteenth centuries. Highly efficient electronic machines are used today to write documents in code, instead of cumbersome manual coding systems. At the end of the nineteenth century, the telephone and the telegraph began to be fundamental tools of diplomatic activity. All of this deeply changed the *modus faciendi* of diplomats but did not change the essence of diplomacy. There are some who argue that all these rapid means of communication decreased the importance of diplomacy. We do not share this opinion, and the facts are increasingly proving it to be ill-founded. What may have reduced at times the importance of diplomacy are the habits of direct communication among statesmen of different countries, which, it is true, have been eased by modern means of communication. But for those political leaders who consider diplomacy an essential instrument and who are less motivated by the demagogic temptation of direct contacts, rapid means of communication, on the contrary, have increased the importance of diplomatic action by rendering it more frequent and convenient. In the final analysis, everything rests on the manner in which those who are responsible for a country's foreign policy choose to exercise their functions.

SECRET AND OPEN DIPLOMACY

The confusion between the concepts of foreign policy and diplomacy, which we are constantly pointing out, is also responsible for the false concept of a secret diplomacy as opposed to an open or public diplomacy.

What is called especially in the American literature secret diplomacy in almost all cases is nothing but secret foreign policy, that is, agreements, understandings, or arrangements between governments that are kept secret from the public. President Wilson, who was, by the way, a professor of political science, bears most responsibilities for this misunderstanding about secret diplomacy, to which were attributed many of the evils leading to World War I. The first of his famous Fourteen Points, proclaimed on January 8, 1918, mentioned the need to celebrate in the future "open covenants openly arrived at" and that "diplomacy should proceed always frankly and in the public view." Harold Nicolson, who as a young diplomat was present at the peace negotiations that ended World War I, remarks that upon his arrival in Paris Wilson immediately made clear that by "diplomacy" he meant not "negotiation," but only the results of this negotiation, that is, the treaties. He also made clear that the expressions "openly arrived at" and "in the public view" were relative and contained nothing that might prevent him from conducting long secret negotiations with Lloyd George and Clemenceau while an American marine kept guard over his office door and another patrolled the small adjacent garden.[4]

This episode elucidates perfectly the problem we are treating. Conceptual confusion led to much talk of secret diplomacy and its evils, while it should have been called secret foreign policy or secret agreements. A politician with President Wilson's responsibilities, leader of a great democratic nation, who had taken upon himself the mission of defending democratic ideals against the prepotency of empires, had to denounce the supposed secret diplomacy, that is, secret agreements or arrangements between governments. Confronted with the requirements of an important and delicate negotiation, he was forced to defend the secrecy of negotiation.

Jules Cambon, once again, made clear that diplomacy or negotiations are secret by nature without this meaning that the right of peoples to know what their governments have committed themselves to is thereby infringed. As Cambon remarks, governments today are, in effect, forced to take public opinion into account but it is a huge step to conclude from there that they should negotiate publicly. "If negotiation were no longer to be secret—he says—there would not be any negotiation at all."[5] And he adds: "If there is secrecy in negotiation, this secrecy ends in the very hour when these negotiations lead to a convention; all things considered, there is no truly secret diplomacy."[6] It is curious to note that D. Francisco de Almeida, Minister of Foreign Affairs of Portugal, in a report presented to the Parliament in 1826 said: "If the good of the State requires that current business be carried on silently for some time, there comes however a time when mystery is not only unnecessary but even criminal."[7] This was said almost a century before President Wilson's Fourteen Points!

It is appropriate to add some other observations made by Jules Cambon about this matter. He said:

A negotiation is like a conversation: none of the participants is free to publish any part of it without thereby harming or offending the other participant. To show the public the adversary's hesitations, transactions, strokes and counter-strokes is to blow bridges behind him and often behind yourself as well and to expose yourself, almost surely, to a total collapse of the process.[8]

On a practical level, the following episode is quite illustrative. In 1963, Senator J. William Fulbright, upset because of the seemingly unending Soviet-American negotiations about a nuclear test ban, gave the following advice to the Secretary of State in Congress:

I rather disagree with the whole procedure you are following—that you try to get agreements of this kind in the open. I think they do not lend themselves to fruitful discussion, if everything the negotiators say has to be addressed to the local constituency back home, rather than to the people participating in the meeting. . . . It seems to me you ought to be able to arrange for negotiations to be private, of course making whatever you conclude public.[9]

Four months after Senator Fulbright's declaration, the talks about a nuclear test ban in effect began to be conducted in secret and Averell Harriman, Viscount Hailsham, and Andrei Gromyko concluded an agreement banning all tests except underground ones.

The author who mentions this episode has written an interesting book about the techniques of international negotiations in which he says the following:

Much has been written about the merits of secret versus open negotiations since the Wilsonian injunction against secret diplomacy. Although Harold Nicolson and other writers have done a service in debunking the strictures against secret bargaining, both the advocates of secrecy and those of openness have gone too far in making such a clear-cut distinction between these two forms of diplomacy— one of them being the right way and the other being wicked. Secrecy is a matter of degree. Negotiations are often kept partly secret. The discussions between the diplomats may not be revealed, but enough about the basic demands and offers may become known to stimulate domestic pressures for changes in the government's position. At times, the mere fact that negotiations take place about a certain issue may be sufficient to lead to uneasiness and protest among certain groups and arouse impatient demands by others that an agreement be concluded. This kind of public reaction all depends on the way in which the news media reports the semi-secret negotiations.[10]

Although these words hold much truth in them, they need a few corrections and explanations. Once again, it is necessary to stress that a secret foreign policy should not be confused with secret diplomacy. On the other hand, according to our definition of the concept of diplomacy, diplomacy and negotiations also should not be identified without certain restrictions. If by negotiation we mean, as the quoted text means, talks or discussions with the precise goal of concluding a certain agreement about a given problem, this activity is but a part of diplomatic activity. Thus, we have to distinguish three entirely different aspects:

1. Whether there should or should not be a secret foreign policy, that is agreements or arrangements between different states unknown to their respective peoples. Such a secret foreign policy has long been rejected by internationalists and politicians, at least in countries where the democratic conception of social life is dominant.

2. Whether diplomatic action should or should not be secret, if we understand diplomacy as being an instrument of foreign policy. Given the variety of types of diplomatic action, it makes no sense to talk about secret diplomacy. A detailed analysis of the diverse components of diplomatic activity will readily make this clear. For example, when a diplomat represents his country in an official act in a foreign country, he acts publicly. But, on the other hand, it must be stressed that a diplomat, in his contacts with the authorities of the country to which he is accredited, with his colleagues, or with other entities, must necessarily keep in the great majority of cases a deep reserve about his conversations, for otherwise he may not only undermine a given action that is being undertaken or studied but also, more seriously, undercut completely his future capacity to perform his role, since those with whom he must stay in contact will henceforth maintain an absolute reserve for fear that whatever will be said to the diplomat will come to public light, compromising interests they must try to satisfy or protect. The fact that mutual trust is crucial to the full exercise of diplomatic activity is something that journalists, politicians, and the public at large often have trouble understanding, since all of them, for different reasons, want to know—and think themselves entitled to know—everything that is going on.

3. Finally, the third aspect is whether negotiations, in the strict sense of talks whose object is the conclusion of a given agreement, should or should not be secret. Regarding this point, Fred Charles Iklé's remarks are correct, since there is obviously a question of degree regarding the amount of secrecy or publicity that should be given to a negotiation or to certain aspects of it. However, Cambon's already quoted words should not be forgotten. It is not possible to negotiate in public. The success of many, indeed most, negotiations derives from the

fact that, at least during certain phases, they were kept secret until the agreement that was reached was publicly unveiled.

Lastly, it is worth remarking that in a given negotiation one of the parties may be interested in making known to the public a certain aspect or detail. Although it is an improper practice that should be avoided by the professional negotiator, in practice it often happens that one of the negotiating parties manufactures an indiscretion or leak to gain an advantage.

By the way of conclusion, we would say that fatuous talk of secret diplomacy and open diplomacy not only makes no sense, but also that such expressions contain a set of false ideas, some of which are dangerous and have caused no little damage to international life and even to the domestic politics of certain countries.

BILATERAL AND MULTILATERAL DIPLOMACY

As we already said, there are peaceful instruments of foreign policy that can be of a unilateral or plurilateral character. Diplomacy is among the latter, and it can be bilateral, if it takes place between the representatives of two states, or multilateral, if it is collective, taking place between the representatives of several states in conferences or international organizations.

The Italian diplomat Adolfo Maresca, who has devoted a large body of work to diplomatic law, prefers to call multilateral diplomacy *plurilateral diplomacy* in his textbook about the subject.[11] We would rather use the normal expression multilateral diplomacy in opposition to bilateral diplomacy, since it seems to us that plurilateral is the opposite of unilateral and plurilateral can be both bilateral and multilateral. The idea of plurality can be applied to two parts only, and therefore include bilateral diplomacy; multilateral suggests the existence of many parts, and therefore it is more appropriate to oppose it to bilateral.

However, disregarding now these terminological differences whose importance, in the final analysis, is not fundamental, we must note at once that the distinction between bilateral diplomacy and multilateral diplomacy is a real distinction in many and varied aspects, unlike those we have already examined.

First, multilateral diplomacy is based on the acknowledgment by a group of countries that they have certain common interests that must be treated jointly.

Second, the elements that constitute diplomatic activity acquire a different importance and relevance in bilateral and multilateral diplomacy.

Third, multilateral diplomacy requires a different technique from that which is used in bilateral diplomacy, since operative conditions are different. Issues are discussed by several representatives seated around a table, therefore requiring particular ways of acting. The creation, particularly after World War I, of international organizations, where the representatives of different countries met regularly to discuss problems of common interest and sometimes to agree on collective solutions, and the structural complexity of some of these organizations led to the development of an entire technique of multilateral diplomacy. True experts in multilateral diplomacy act similarly in many ways to parliamentary politicians in international organizations of universal scope and primarily political character.

According to Dean Rusk, who seems to have been the first to use this expression, that form of multilateral diplomacy used in the United Nations and its specialized agencies would be parliamentary diplomacy, which, by the way is the title of an interesting study by Philip Jessup.[12] While it is a fact that the diplomacy of the United Nations has some particular characteristics, we do not consider, however, that it is different enough to have created a type of diplomacy essentially different from the rest of multilateral diplomacy.

But, if, in fact, there exists a multilateral diplomacy that can be distinguished from the usual bilateral diplomacy, this does not mean that one is opposed to the other, in the sense that one can substitute for the existence of the other. Thus some authors argue nonsensically that bilateral diplomacy, which they call classic no longer exists, having been substituted by multilateral diplomacy, which they also call modern diplomacy. Nothing could be more erroneous and contrary to reality.

Bilateral diplomacy not only performs functions impossible to carry out through multilateral diplomacy, as we shall see more clearly when we analyze the diverse elements of diplomatic activity, but multilateral diplomacy itself cannot function without resorting to bilateral diplomacy. It is an illusion to think that in a conference or in an international organization everything can be discussed, arranged, or solved around a table at which all participants are present, or in small, more-or-less tight little groups of countries. Important bilateral contacts always take place, and the representatives to these conferences or international organizations must often resort to bilateral representations made by their own countries to ease their task in these conferences or international organizations. Sometimes these bilateral representations are the decisive element in a given multilateral decision. For this reason, governments that wish to obtain a given result, for example in an international organization, almost always support the action of their representatives in that organization with bilateral representations to some or all member states. Therefore, bilateral and multilateral diplomacy complement each other and, contrary to what some authors say, multilateral diplomacy has not diminished the importance of bilateral diplomacy, but rather the opposite. Concerning this matter, we will quote the words of Ambassador Nascimento e Silva, who was director of the Rio Branco Institute:

Even at the United Nations, where decisions are supposedly taken in the plenary, as a result of the speeches that were made and of the debates that took place, the fact is that diplomacy, and not speeches and votes, has the last word in solving problems and that the distinction between parliamentary diplomacy and quiet diplomacy is known and practiced ever more. Those who served at the United Nations know the processes that Secretary General Hammarskjöld called quiet diplomacy, which are continuously used in the corridors and ballrooms, in receptions, luncheons and dinners, and in the offices and residences of the representatives. Dag Hammarskjöld had the opportunity to defend the secrecy of informations exchanged in those contacts, stressing that "no member-State has the right to know the content of my interviews. If, for example, I have a talk with the representatives of the Pakistani government, the government of India has no right to know from me information about that talk. We cannot allow everything to be discussed by the press."[13]

DIPLOMACY AND LAW

Some superficial resemblances between the activities of a diplomatic agent and those of a lawyer have led some to think that the two activities, if not identical, are at least close. The fact that many diplomats, today as well as in the past, have been trained in the law field naturally has tended to worsen the trend to exaggerate the parallels between the two activities, even leading some diplomats who have such training to hold a mistaken view of their profession. A diplomat should, in truth, have some basic notions of law, and the lawyer should have a certain skill for negotiation and compromise. But their situations are different, and their professional training is oriented by different principles and conditions.

The situations of a diplomat and a lawyer are essentially different. In the typical situation in which lawyers usually find themselves involved, for example in a court, A tries to show C that B is not right, and B tries to show C that A is not right; C, whose interests are not involved, must make the final decision about who is right. In a typical diplomatic situation, A tries to convince B that he is right (or rather, that his government is right) and vice versa. Moreover, both A and B represent sovereign entities. It could be observed that there are international courts, whose task is to settle disputes between states. But when states decide to submit a dispute to one of these courts, diplomatic action stops, and the case is argued on juridical grounds, by lawyers and according to a juridical process.

On the other hand, as Ambassador Charles Thayer says, the training of a lawyer accustoms him to presuppose the existence of a court, in which what is just and lawful is distinct from what is unjust and unlawful, and the existence of a police force and prisons to enforce the decisions of the court.

However, diplomacy does not try to ascertain what is just and unjust but rather to accommodate different or conflicting interests.[14] Diplomats act essentially in the political field where political considerations are paramount. They act on a plane different and higher than that of lawyers, which is the protection of private interests within a well-defined legal framework.

Thus, insofar as a diplomat acts exclusively or mainly as a lawyer, he negates or betrays the very essence of diplomacy.

DIPLOMACY AND BUSINESS

Since diplomacy is often involved with business affairs, it may seem at first sight that diplomatic activity has a great affinity with the activity of businessmen. This idea is particularly widespread in certain American circles. The experienced American diplomat Charles Thayer says about this matter:

It is widely believed, particularly in America, that diplomatic negotiations are essentially business deals and that the best negotiator is therefore a shrewd Yankee horse trader operating under the cover of a pair of striped pants. As a result, a number of successful businessmen without diplomatic experience have found themselves pantless and shirtless at the end of a negotiation with experienced diplomats.[15]

The same author explains that, in fact, diplomatic negotiations are fundamentally different from business negotiations.

In the first place, business, like the law, is conducted within the framework of a regulated system with self-enforcing powers. Business to a large extent is regulated by the law of contracts. Even international business deals generally provide for arbitration in the court of one or the other contracting party. Diplomacy has been defined as "commerce in mutual benefit" or the harmonizing of interests. Only as long as mutual benefits accrue or harmony prevails is there any real assurance that the agreements will be fulfilled.[16]

We would add that the training of businessmen to defend narrow private interests is certainly neither an adequate nor a useful training for the defense of public interests, especially when businessmen are up against persons experienced in the diplomatic field.

Chapter 4

DIPLOMATIC PATHOLOGY

BACKCHANNEL DIPLOMACY

Let us examine now the deviations from normal diplomatic practice that frequently occur, which we shall call *diplomatic pathology*. One of them is the use by holders of political power of an alternative channel to the official diplomatic channel. That alternative channel is often called a backchannel, and therefore we shall call this deviation *backchannel diplomacy*. Another notorious deviation does not concern the normal means of diplomacy but its normal end, that is, the maintenance and development of peaceful relations between states. This deviation consists in using diplomacy as a tool in the ideological struggle and for creating, temporarily or permanently, a tense situation between certain states. We will call this deviation from normal diplomatic practice *combat diplomacy*. Another such deviation is the use of diplomacy for obtaining secret information or information gathered by illicit means. We will call it *diplomatic intelligence and counter-intelligence*.

The holders of political power, in their contacts with the political authorities of other states, are often tempted to use personal channels that are independent from the official or diplomatic channels. Unable or unwilling to establish direct contact, and sometimes even acknowledging the drawbacks of this method, they use intermediaries but not the official intermediaries accredited for that purpose, namely diplomatic agents. What are the reasons for this abnormality, for an abnormality it is? The reasons are varied. Sometimes, the reason is pure personal vanity: the political entity wishes to personally solve a certain problem, or at least, make it seem so, bypassing the official machinery that exists for this purpose, with which it does not want to share any part of the credit in case of success. The reason can also be the promotion of hidden interests, which can range from purely material interests to political or party interests, requiring treatment outside normal official channels. Another reason may be the lack of political or professional trust in the diplomatic agents in certain posts. All of these reasons and others may easily lead holders of political power into the temptation of accepting or seeking the services of an entity outside the normal official circuit to establish international contacts, especially if this entity has strong credentials, such as, for example, an intimate knowledge of the country where he or she is to act or personal links with the holders of political power of that country, with their families, or with influential individuals.

The results produced by the use of such backchannels are almost always illusory and even counter-productive. In the great majority of cases, the loss of prestige to the official diplomatic representative resulting inevitably from the use of a backchannel does not serve the national interest. Except in the case of very young states or those with a weak political and administrative development, where personal power is sometimes stronger than institutional power, unofficial agents do not by themselves achieve useful results, even if they are very well received. Unofficial agents, even when they are well-received, do not by themselves achieve useful results for their countries. Formality has an almost unsurpassable force in relations between states, although this may not be easily perceived by those who, for personal reasons, wish to use nonofficial channels.

Thus it is not surprising to hear Sir Alexander Cadogan, Secretary-General of the British Foreign Office during World War II, comment acidly about Winston Churchill's personal representative to King Leopold of Belgium, Admiral Roger Keyes: "Why send these ridiculous unofficial busybody's 'emissaries'? They don't know the background, so they don't understand and they can't report correctly, because they're not trained to."[1]

As we already observed, the use of backchannels to advance merely personal interests, whatever they may be, cannot but run counter to national interests. If, however, backchannels are used to advance inequivocably national interests because of a lack of confidence in the normal official agents, this may seem a practice that, even if it has certain drawbacks, is acceptable or, at least, excusable. We do not, however, accept this conclusion since, in such cases, the only proper solution is the replacement of the official agent. In exceptional cases, when the urgency of the matter allows no time to undertake this replacement, an alternative agent can be used, but even in this case it is always possible to avoid using a backchannel, by using instead a special envoy, accredited for that effect for a limited period through the normal diplomatic representatives. Therefore, the use of backchannels can never be justified, and, almost always, it can only be explained by hidden personal interests.

An important distinction must still be made in this delicate matter of backchannel diplomacy. Backchannels can be used by the political organ that, constitutionally, has legitimacy to conduct the foreign policy of a given state. Sometimes, however, albeit not very frequently, backchannels are used by political organs that have no such legitimacy. These cases constitute a most serious diplomatic pathology that should not be called simply backchannel diplomacy but illegitimate backchannel diplomacy. The distinction is important because, although backchannel diplomacy properly speaking has many drawbacks, it still is a legitimate process, whereas in the other case, there is a usurping of power with grave consequences both in the external and internal fields. In the external field, the cardinal principle of unity in the conduct of foreign policy is violated with serious consequences for the defense of state interests. In the internal field, conflicts between the political organs naturally arise, troubling the normal functioning of state machinery.

COMBAT DIPLOMACY

As we already said, the aim of diplomacy is to maintain and develop good relations between states and to solve peacefully the conflicts or differences that may arise between them. Certain states, however, use diplomacy as an instrument of ideological penetration in other countries or as a tool for maintaining a state of international tension that is convenient for domestic political reasons. Both cases naturally constitute a deviation from normal diplomatic practice belonging to a true diplomatic pathology.

Although many and varied instance of this abnormal type of diplomacy could be cited, the most obvious one, which foreign policy experts have compiled most evidence of, is the case of the Soviet Union, whose diplomatic practice tries to achieve an effect of ideological penetration and serves, in certain instances, to maintain international tensions required by domestic imperatives.

Regarding the former aspect, ideological penetration or expansion, we will quote a Soviet textbook on international law: "In the Soviet Union . . . diplomacy for the first time in the history of mankind wholly serves the interests of the working people, not only of the USSR, but also of all other countries."[2] Another Soviet textbook on diplomacy says about the same theme and also concerning the struggle against non-communist countries (called imperialists):

[Communist diplomacy] is invariably successful in exposing the aggressive intentions of the imperialist governments. . . . It does this from the tribunes of diplomatic conferences, in official diplomatic statements and documents, as well as in the press. This is one of the important methods of socialist diplomacy by means of which it mobilizes democratic social opinion and the masses of people all over the world against the aggressive policies of the imperialist governments.[3]

The reasons for such uses of diplomacy lie deep in the ancient history of the Russian people, as we shall see more clearly later on, but they also have a more immediate and up-to-date explanation in the very structure of the Soviet system. George Kennan, an expert on Soviet foreign policy, remarks, in a famous essay, that the process of political consolidation of the Soviet regime "has never been completed and the men in the Kremlin have continued to be predominantly absorbed with the struggle to secure and make absolute the power which they seized in November 1917." And he adds:

Since capitalism no longer existed in Russia and since it would not be admitted that there could be serious or widespread opposition to the Kremlin springing spontaneously from the liberated masses under its authority, it became necessary to justify the retention of the dictatorship by stressing the menace of capitalism abroad. This began at an early date. In 1924, Stalin specifically defended the retention of the "organs of suppression," meaning, among others, the army and the secret police, on the ground that "as long as there is a capitalist encirclement there will be danger of intervention with all the consequences that flow from that danger."[4]

Analyzing Soviet foreign policy in greater depth, Vernon Aspaturian, professor at Pennsylvania State University and a noted expert on Soviet politics, remarks,

The social and institutional groups in Soviet society which appear to benefit from an aggressive foreign policy and the maintenance of international tensions are (1) the armed forces, (2) the heavy-industrial managers, (3) professional party *apparatchiki* and ideologues. . . . The professional military, on the whole, has a natural interest in a large and modern military establishment and a high priority on budget and resources: the heavy-industrial managerial groups have a vested interest in preserving the primacy of their sector of the economy; and the Party apparatus traditionally has had a vested interest in ideological conformity and the social controls which they rationalized, thus ensuring the primacy of the apparatus over all other social forces in the Soviet system. All these functional roles are served best under conditions of international tension. Consequently, these groups wittingly or unwittingly have developed a vested interest in either maintaining international tensions or creating the illusion of insecurity and external danger, which would produce the same effect.[5]

Soviet diplomacy, thus, has truly been conceived as a combat diplomacy, which naturally constitutes a deviation from normality as defined by our concept of diplomacy. Neither is it surprising that this combat diplomacy has also been an agressive and sometimes quite rude diplomacy. This agressiveness and rudeness naturally shocked old-guard-diplomats, such as Lord Vansittart, who was Secretary General of the British Foreign Office for many years before World War II. He wrote the following words about this matter in 1950.

Nowadays the diplomacy of an increasing part of the world is thoughtfully calculated to create and maintain *bad* relations. This, of course, is done in no mere *Schadenfreude* or spirit of spite. Bad relations with western democracies and capitalist countries are an article of faith, an accepted condition for the survival of Totalitaria. The successful Communist statesman is therefore he who ensures the permanence and intensity of this condition. So the missions of the Cominform are largely stocked with persons who make no pretense of practising diplomacy as previously defined, but are employed solely for hostile propaganda, sabotage, subversion and espionage. I have plenty of evidence and illustration for which I have no space here, and which indeed are unnecessary to demonstrate so notorious a truism.[6]

Vansittart's attitude is a natural one for a diplomat of the old guard, as we said, and his explanation of the aggressive diplomacy practiced by the Soviet Union coincides in the main with those put forward by the experts on Soviet politics already quoted. His conclusions, however, seem to us exaggerated, since he considers this fact to be evidence for the decline of diplomacy. We find this conclusion unacceptable, because the pathological manifestations of diplomacy that we pointed out, and others that may have escaped us, do not invalidate true diplomacy. The enormous expansion of international relations that occurred in the postwar period shows the expansion and not the decline of diplomacy, as we shall see further ahead when criticisms of diplomacy and its supposed crisis will be dealt with.

Although the Soviet Union is not the only country to make abnormal use of diplomacy, we dealt with in particular because, as we said, it is the best known and most important case, about which more elements of study are available. It is curious to note that relevant historical reasons can be found in the history of the Russian people that help to explain Soviet behavior in the field of foreign relations, as is the case with many other matters relating to Soviet politics. As was said above, the Russians always considered themselves to be the great cultural inheritors of the Byzantine empire, which made great use of diplomacy as a tool for provoking and maintaining dissensions between its neighboring peoples. "The chief occupation of envoys dispatched by Constantinople," Charles Thayer reminds us, "was not to foster peace and friendship but to foment feuds and rivalries between the tribes on the outer borders of the empire."[7] As we already said when dealing with the diplomacy of the Byzantine empire, the rudeness and haughtiness of the diplomats themselves always was an Oriental and Byzantine tradition, whose principles, by the way, were already expressed in the *Arthasastra*, of the Brahmin Kautilyas, written in the fourth century B.C.

DIPLOMATIC INTELLIGENCE AND COUNTER-INTELLIGENCE

As we shall see, one of the constituent elements of diplomatic activity is information collected by lawful means. When it is gathered by unlawful means, the activity of gathering it can no longer be considered to be normal diplomatic practice, but rather intelligence or espionage.

However, it sometimes happens that professional diplomats perform intelligence activities in the countries to which they are accredited. This naturally is a grave deviation from their normal functions. Most frequently, intelligence and counter-intelligence agents are stationed in diplomatic missions under cover of diplomatic statute. These deviations from normal diplomatic practice happen especially in the diplomatic representations of the superpowers and the most important other countries.

We will treat this matter in greater depth when we deal with the informative role of diplomacy.

Chapter 5

CRITICISMS OF DIPLOMACY AND THE CRISIS OF DIPLOMACY

CRITICISMS OF DIPLOMACY

We have seen how the confusion between the concepts of foreign policy and diplomacy has led to false criticisms of diplomacy, whose targets were in fact the foreign policies of this or that country, in this or that period. This does not mean, however, that serious and general critiques of diplomacy do not exist. These critiques come not only from the field of journalism or from non-experts but also from experts in the field of political science. Talk of a crisis of diplomacy is also heard often, but with widely different meanings. Let us look more closely at these two aspects.

Concerning the critique of diplomacy, we shall deal with the critique made by George Modelski, professor of political science in Washington University of Seattle, in his book *Principles of World Politics*, for three reasons: first, because this book comes from the field of political science; second, because its critique of diplomacy is aimed at the very existence of the diplomatic institution; and third, because it is the most thorough and demolishing critique of diplomacy we know of. However, a preliminary warning about this author's critique is needed: on the one hand, he considers bilateral diplomacy as classic diplomacy, or, in other words, the diplomacy of the past, and multilateral diplomacy as the modern and future diplomacy, his criticisms being directed against the former; on the other hand, he does not favor the nation-state system in which we

live, and he develops the principles of a worldwide political
system that would substitute and surpass that system. Given
this, the author makes the following criticisms of bilateral diplomacy:

a) The practice of resident diplomatic missions was instituted at a
time when communications, even over short European distances, were
unreliable and expensive. . . . But today, communications are in-
stant, worldwide, cheap and secure. . . . Are diplomats still filling a
real need?[1]

Concerning this criticism, we may begin by observing that
resident diplomatic missions began to proliferate in the sixteenth century, as we saw, putting down roots mainly in the
next century. Difficulties of communication were certainly not
the determining element in the creation of the system of permanent missions or resident ambassadors, since those difficulties, and even bigger ones, existed in previous times, when
diplomatic missions had a temporary character. Moreover, the
fact that diplomatic missions acquired a permanent character
did not thereby alter the material difficulties of communication between the countries that sent or received these missions. Following this line of thought, it is not our modern rapid
means of communication that can make permanent diplomatic missions unnecessary, as will be clear further ahead.
Obviously, the point of departure for this line of criticism is
the false notion that these missions serve only for relaying
information and that direct communication between the political leaders of the different states is more advantageous than
communication through intermediaries.

Finally, the same author begins by doubting the need for
permanent missions and ends by asking whether diplomats
still fill a real need. Now, one thing is the need for permanent
missions and another the need for diplomacy. As we saw, there
has been a need for diplomacy for thousands of years, long
before permanent missions existed. This system has been in
place in a generalized manner for only three or four centuries,
which shows that, whether or not there are permanent missions, there continues to be a need for diplomacy. The system
of permanent missions has been criticized even by professional diplomats, at least in certain cases and in the general

manner in which it is used today. But this does not mean that
resident missions ought to be abolished entirely and much less
so that bilateral diplomatic representations should be aban-
doned. We will come back to this matter further ahead and
discuss it in greater detail.

b) As a century-old and tradition-bound institution, diplomacy has
been consistently resistant to technological innovation. The typewriter . . . encountered resistance in the great offices of state, where
the belief in the efficacy of finely penned notes persisted long after
the speed and efficiency of the typewriter had been demonstrated
beyond any doubt. . . . The telephone remains almost totally unu-
tilized in interstate relations.[2]

This type of criticism mainly reveals a surprising ignorance
of the way in which foreign departments of state nowadays
function, at least those of the most important or highly developed countries. If the typewriter, for example, met with some
resistance in diplomatic services when its use became widespread at the beginning of this century, such resistance was
not a phenomenon peculiar to these services, but rather a
common reaction of all bureaucracies, which are generally
hostile to technological innovation. But from the moment when
the use of typewriters became widespread in public services,
it was also adopted by the diplomatic services. As a parenthesis, we should add that the author of this criticism is mistaken when he supposes that, as he says, "The speed and efficiency of the typewriter has been demonstrated beyond any
doubt in commerce and industry." Experts in the field of man-
agement services have long come to the conclusion that the
generalized use of typewriters has certain drawbacks in terms
of costs and efficiency and that for certain types of interser-
vice communications, for example, handwritten messages are
preferable.

As for the reduced use of the telephone in the international
communications of diplomatic services, the author of this criticism is also ill-informed. Its use is so generalized that some
central diplomatic offices have been forced to establish strict
rules for the use of telephones. Moreover, contrary to what
the author of these criticisms says, the use of electronic ma-

chines has also invaded diplomatic services, particularly the coding services.

c) It must be remembered that the diplomatic system was originally instituted not so much to improve communications, but rather to replace one intimate communications system with another more impersonal system. The Middle Ages constituted, in Europe, a period of great 'togetherness'. . . . The new system of diplomatic representation therefore grew out of the need to keep *political leaders apart*. It instituted the barrier of intermediaries. It is . . . a well-tried system for *minimizing* interaction, and for keeping people apart, instead of bringing them together.[3]

Modelski's observations are faulty because they lack historical basis and spring from a mistaken point of view about the function of diplomacy. As we already saw, diplomacy is an institution thousands of years old, found even in primitive societies. Taking into account the serious drawbacks of direct contacts between leaders of different political units, which were mentioned more than once, diplomacy, or the use of intermediaries, has served to maintain connections between these leaders and not to keep them apart, as Modelski says. His conclusion results from the false premise that he adopts that direct contacts between political leaders are the best way to solve problems between two or more nations, something which is utterly disproved by history. Considering only recent cases, it will suffice to mention the disastrous results of the personal intervention of President Wilson in the Paris Peace Conference of 1919 and the conferences of Munich in 1938 and Yalta in 1945, which were conducted at the highest level. Incidentally, when Modelski refers to the frequent contacts between princes in the Middle Ages, he does not produce any evidence as to the advantages of such contacts for the concerned peoples. Moreover, as the famous medievalist François Ganshof remarks, most negotiations in the Middle Ages were conducted by envoys representing the respective sovereigns.[4] On the other hand, contrary to what the author of these criticisms implies, direct contacts between political leaders of different states have multiplied in number in the postwar period, but their results have certainly not been more productive or encouraging than those achieved by the old diplomatic institution. About this point, it is appropriate to remind the reader of the opinions of two former American secretaries of state, Dean Acheson and Dean Rusk, who were both politicians and not diplomats.[5]

Modelski says lastly,

d) As a communication function diplomacy today is without any importance. The world's press is fully adequate to the task of reporting general political and economic developments in all areas. . . . Characteristic of the distrustful spirit of diplomacy is the story, probably apocryphal, that is attributed to Metternich, the master diplomat: upon being told of the death of the Russian Ambassador at the Congress of Vienna, he exclaimed, "Ah, is that true? What could have been his motive?" Diplomats, like intelligence organizations, see the world as composed of fragments only; they never see the world as one, and they lack either the incentive or even the conceptual equipment to develop ideas of world interest.[6]

The very language in which this criticism is couched denotes its lack of objectivity. The author could have said that diplomacy has little importance as a system of communication; but instead he states it has none. He could have said that the international press makes an important or significant contribution to the task of informing governments; but he says instead that the press is fully adequate to perform this function; concerning this we could confine ourselves to quoting Talleyrand: "*Tout ce qui est exageré est négligeable.*" But we would rather analyze these criticisms against diplomacy in greater depth because of the ease with which they are accepted and repeated.

Their author would certainly be surprised with the intense work undertaken every day by diplomatic missions to correct, interpret, and so often deny the news given by the most reputable international press. One does not need to be an expert on the media to know that a large part of the international press is dominated by certain political orientations or by private interests of economic and other groups, making it difficult to accept *prima facie* that the information it carries is objective or impartial. The other, so-called independent press, even if its information is consciously and impartially prepared, always needs a critical analysis that can only be made *in loco*. As a matter of course, this information is produced at great speed, under time pressure, and without great chances of carefully verifying the truthfulness of reported facts, making it impossible for any conscious government to rely for its political analysis only on press information, unless it is corroborated by its official agents abroad. Not to speak, of course, of an unfortunately quite common type of press, which does not hesitate to print the most absurd news without even trying to confirm it, merely to produce a sensation. The archives of all foreign offices throughout the world are full of newspaper clippings containing the most fantastic news, some of which led to an increase in international tensions or even originated conflicts. Recall, for example the role that a certain sensationalist press played in the origins of the Spanish-American War.[7]

As for the superficial or distorted nature of the information given by diplomats, Modelski once again shows himself to be influenced by the old clichés of the superficial and gossipy diplomat created by certain literature. About this matter, we shall quote Harold Nicolson's words in a preface to a book by an American author:

American public opinion has been somewhat bewildered by several often contradictory views of a diplomatist's true function and importance. There are those who regard the Foreign service as a kind of bird sanctuary for elegant young men, with the milk of Groton still wet upon their lips, arrayed in striped pants and spending most of their time handing sugar cookies to ladies of high society in Europe and Latin America. Conversely, there are those who regard diplomatists as an international gang of intriguers intent upon ensnaring the great white soul of the United States.[8]

There certainly can be second or third-class diplomats who send information of little interest and that not always trustworthy, but as a rule they are of little relevance, and their information is filtered by the competent services at headquarters. It should be noted, however, that this is not the main fault of such diplomats; it would rather be the habit of mindlessly following the local press without any critical spirit. These cases, however, do not allow one to make a sweeping and absolute statement about the superficiality and uselessness of diplomatic information and of diplomats themselves. In the same fashion, the fact that some professors lack objectivity and poorly document their work does not allow us to consider the teaching profession useless or harmful. Lastly, many countries have published huge collections of their diplomatic correspondence, which are considered by the experts to be among the most important sources for the history of international relations. The reading of these collections demonstrates precisely the opposite of what Modelski says.

We always heard that great masters have the habit of warning their pupils against hurried generalizations. Modelski, who is prolific in such generalizations, tells an anecdote about Metternich that he himself considers probably apocryphal, and that, at the most, could show Metternich's suspicious nature but more exactly shows his propensity for the blague, in order to conclude that diplomacy is imbued of a sickly spirit of suspicion!

We will also tell a story, albeit a true one, that well illustrates the incongruity of Modelski's arguments about diplomacy and the press. At the time of the First Republic in Portugal, a time of great confusion when one revolution came on the heels of another, a very intelligent young diplomat was chargé d'affaires in Paris, owing to the absence of the chief of mission. The government asked him by telegraph to inquire immediately about the position of the French government in a conference that would take place within a few days. Our second secretary, chargé d'affaires, could not find out anything at the different levels to which he generally had access at the Quai d'Orsay, and therefore, taking courage, decided to ask for an urgent audience, which could not be denied, with the Secretary-General of the Quai d'Orsay. The Secretary-General was an old ambassador, a man of a certain standing but with that supercilious manner sometimes found among high officials of the French administration. He received the poor Portuguese second secretary with a certain annoyance and determined to discourage him from future initiatives as chargé d'affaires. Directly upon the entrance of the second secretary, before asking him to sit down, he asked him in a sarcastic tone how were things going in Portugal and how many deaths had been caused by the last few revolutions. Our young secretary replied without blinking: "A very small percentage of the deaths caused by the French Revolution." Changing his tone at once, the ambassador told him to sit down and asked him what he wanted. The secretary transmitted the request of his government to which the Secretary-General answered dryly: "Buy *Le Temps* tomorrow morning and you will find out about the French position." Our secretary, always calm and collected, stood up and said: "Thank you very much for your suggestion. My government will certainly appreciate it deeply, since it will allow it to make considerable savings." The ambassador frowned and could not resist the temptation to ask him what he meant. The secretary calmly explained: "For, if my government follows your advice, it will certainly close all of its diplomatic missions and instead get a subscription to the major newspapers of the different world capitals." The ambassador, realizing his foolishness, let out a burst of laughter, told him to sit down again, and gave him the information he sought.

Professor Modelski wants to transform this *boutade* of a young diplomat made more than sixty years ago into a serious proposition. In our opinion, his confidence in the informative value of the press should be confronted with a report produced in 1947 by a commission about the freedom of the press, whose chairman and vice-chairman were respectively the dean of the University of Chicago, Robert Hutchins, and a law professor of Harvard University, Zechariah Chafee, Jr. This report says, among other things:

These instruments (press, radio and other means of mass communication) can spread lies faster and farther than our forefathers dreamed when they enshrined the freedom of the press in the First Amendment of the Constitution. . . . The news is twisted by the emphasis on firstness, on the novel and sensational; by the personal interest of the owners; and by the pressure groups.[9]

About Modelski's statement that diplomats have a fragmented vision of the world and that "they lack either the incentive or even the conceptual equipment to develop ideas of world interest," we note once again that the author of this criticism does not produce any evidence or justification for his statement. This fact leads us to suppose that Modelski probably assumes that diplomats necessarily have a fragmented vision of the world because they serve consecutively in several countries. This conclusion, however, is abusive and superficial and does not take into account either the realities of diplomatic life or the individual characteristics of each diplomat per se, since they are far from being manufactured in an assembly line. In fact, for a diplomat stationed in Washington or even in the Vatican, it will be difficult to have a fragmented vision of international life. Moreover, there is no reason why even those who serve their country in Lusaka, Bangkok, or Brasilia should necessarily have a fragmented vision of the world. His statement utterly ignores the fact that diplomats spend a large part of their careers at headquarters, where they generally deal with matters of regional or universal scope; and, moreover, many diplomats who served for years in the bilateral field are then transferred to their countries' delegations to the international organizations, and vice versa; and some are even transferred to the international secretariats of these organizations to occupy important directing posts and at times the chief post itself, as has been the case with the office of Secretary General of such organizations as the UN, the GATT, NATO, and ICAO (General Agreement Trade Tariffs, North Atlantic Treaty Organization, International Civil Aviation Organization). Career diplomats have even played an important role in launching certain political projects of a regional or universal scope. To cite but one example, the Atlantic Charter was drafted by Sir Alexander Cadogan, who was then Secretary General of the British Foreign Office.[10] All these well-known cases prove beyond doubt how devoid of basis is Modelski's statement.

In conclusion, we could say that Modelski's criticisms miss their target because their author, in truth, reveals a complete lack of knowledge of the essence of diplomacy and of its practical functioning. Naturally, diplomacy as an administrative branch of this or that state has many aspects, varying from case to case, that can be strongly criticized. But these shortcomings in terms of organization and functioning have nothing to do with the validity of the institution itself, which is the target for the criticisms we have been examining.

CRISIS OF DIPLOMACY

Nowadays, talk of a crisis of diplomacy is frequently heard. This expression, however, can mean widely different things that ought to be distinguished.

In a very narrow sense, a crisis of diplomacy in this or that country can mean two things: difficulties in the recruitment of diplomatic personnel or the bad quality of the existing diplomatic personnel. These are particular aspects of the diplomatic organization of certain countries, which although important, touch but lightly, if at all, upon a general theory of diplomacy.

If we take the word diplomacy in its general sense, talk of a crisis of diplomacy derives mainly from the fact that diplomatic agents have recently been subject to several acts of violence, having been kidnapped, taken hostage, and even murdered. *Time* magazine dedicated its issue of March 17, 1980, to the "crisis of diplomacy" that, according to this magazine, springs from the terrorist actions directed against diplomats and diplomatic missions in the last few years. According to a report by the Rand Corporation, quoted by that magazine, there were forty-two terrorist attacks against diplomatic missions between 1971 and March 1980. According to *Time* (March 17, 1980), five American ambassadors were murdered between 1969 and 1980; ten Turkish diplomats, or close members of their families, were also murdered between 1973 and 1980, not to mention the failed assassination attempts. As everybody knows, several diplomats of various nationalities were subject not long ago to kidnappings and incarceration, as was the case with the fifty American diplomats and mission personnel in Teheran and with fifteen ambassadors (including the representative of the Holy See) imprisoned in the Dominican embassy in Bogota.

These attacks against diplomatic missions or diplomatic agents can be taken as an indication of, or evidence for, a crisis of diplomacy only by deplorably confused thinking. To begin with, the terrorist attacks against diplomatic agents and missions are not aimed at the diplomatic institution itself, but they are rather ways of trying to force certain authorities to take certain measures or to make certain payments. If the targets of terrorists were bankers instead of diplomats (which, by the way, has already happened), nobody would think of saying that the banking institution was in crisis, just as no one would say that the Roman Catholic Church is in crisis because the pope was the target of an assassination attempt.

In the cases of attempts against diplomatic representatives and missions, there is a crisis not of diplomacy but of state authority. The urban terrorism of today brought to light a contemporary phenomenon, more or less widespread from country to country: the crisis of authority confronting the democratic state of today, which renders it almost impotent to avoid, prevent, or punish terrorist attacks.

If diplomacy is taken as a generalized institution, there is said to be a crisis of diplomacy in that the great technical progress in the field of communications and the frequent meetings between the political leaders of the several states have diminished the importance of diplomacy. We have said enough about the advantages and efficacy of direct meetings between statesmen to return now to this matter. But, if it is true that, independently of their results, these contacts have increased in number in recent times, it is equally true that diplomatic representations have also progressively increased in number instead of decreasing, something which denotes the progress and not the decline of diplomatic activity. A century ago, there were no more than a few hundred diplomatic missions throughout the world, whereas today there are about seven thousand embassies representing about 150 countries.[11] In a way, it is ridiculous to speak in this sense of a crisis of diplomacy when in fact we have been witnessing an explosion of diplomacy. This explosion of diplomacy has naturally created a problem of personnel, which is felt with greater acuity in this or that country, particularly in those that gained independence only recently or in those that, having a small diplomatic service, were forced to expand it in a hurry. It is obvious that the quality of the diplomatic agent has declined, as a rule, relatively to the diplomatic personnel of the period prior to World War II. In this sense, it is possible to speak of a crisis of diplomatic personnel, which, however, should not be confused with a crisis of the diplomatic institution.

Another aspect of this supposed crisis of diplomacy has been raised by professional diplomats themselves. In a article published in *The Times* of London on January 15, 1980, the Italian ambassador Roberto Ducci raised doubts about the need to keep permanent diplomatic missions, asking whether in fact it would not be better to abolish them, using instead temporary embassies as was the practice prior to the sixteenth century. The point now is whether there is a crisis of the permanent diplomatic mission and not of diplomacy. Ambassador Ducci argues that embassies in friendly countries are useless and those in hostile countries risky.

Although there are valid arguments against the excessive proliferation of permanent diplomatic missions, in many cases they still answer an imperative need, due to the innumerable interests existing between certain countries that require constant and routine care. Therefore, we do not believe it possible to abolish permanent missions, replacing them by temporary or ad hoc missions. The problem, therefore, can be reduced to knowing how extensive a network of permanent representations should each country have, a matter that can only be resolved case by case, according to the circumstances of each country.

In a general way, it can be said that many permanent missions do not in fact answer an imperative need of this or that state, but were created and are maintained for reasons of prestige, of a kind which is illusory or of a purely domestic effect. In countries with limited financial means and a small number of officials trained for the diplomatic service, it is a grave mistake to increase excessively the number of permanent missions for the illusory reason of maintaining a prestige that does not in fact accrue from the mere creation of such missions. Diplomatic representations with little personnel and small means do not make it possible to reap the prestige claimed internally. It is ridiculous to think that prestige will accrue to a country that sends abroad an ambassador manufactured in a hurry, who sometimes does not even have other diplomatic officials to help him and who is improperly lodged, being for all these reasons unable to compete with the majority of his or her foreign colleagues. In these circumstances, it would be preferable, of course, to concentrate the financial means and the available personnel in permanent missions of fundamental interest and to reduce the number of permanent representations by accrediting some ambassadors in two or three places.

In the special cases of the member-states of a community of states with the final goal of political integration, as is the case with the European Economic Community (EEC), it is understandable that the importance of the respective diplomatic representations will tend to decrease as this integration progresses, until the optimal point is reached when diplomatic representations die a natural death because political integration is complete. We do not believe, however, that the state of evolution of political integration within the EEC has reached a point where the importance of the respective diplomatic representations of its members has been drastically reduced. Roberto Ducci's observations, even if applied only to the case of the EEC, seem to us exaggerated.

ANALYSIS OF DIPLOMATIC ACTIVITY

CONSTITUENT ELEMENTS OF DIPLOMATIC ACTIVITY

Diplomatic activity, or the activity of diplomatic agents, consists of multiple elements, ranging from actions of a purely representational character, for example, participating in an official act, to the negotiation of highly complex international agreements.

The need to regulate in juridical terms the functions of diplomatic missions led, in the field of international law, to a listing of the main elements of diplomatic activity. In this respect, as in others pertaining to diplomacy, law has gone further than political science. These elements, which will be examined in detail further ahead, are listed in the Vienna Convention on Diplomatic Relations of April 18, 1961, as: a) representation; b) protection; c) information; d) promotion; e) negotiation.

The listing made in the Vienna Convention is not exhaustive, allowing, therefore, for the existence of other unlisted elements. If, for example, a citizen of State A living in or passing through State B goes to the consular section of State A's embassy to request the services of a notary public, in which element of diplomatic activity should these services be included? It is certainly not protection, if this concept is taken in the precise sense, which will be explained later. Rather, it is a public service available to any citizen of State A but performed for his or her convenience in State B, where he is living or passing through. It is therefore an extension abroad of the public services of a given state, services which are then performed in another state. These services can be of several types, comprising, along with the already mentioned notarial acts, acts of civil registrar or relating to the military draft, electoral registration, passport or visa provision, and so on.

This extension abroad of public services, performed by consular services, which can be autonomous consulates or consular sections of diplomatic missions, is not specifically included in the listing of functions attributed to diplomatic missions made by the Vienna Convention on Diplomatic Relations, because it is dealt with in another international agreement, the Vienna Convention on Consular Relations, signed on April 24, 1963.

In juridical terms, diplomatic and consular functions are distinct activities, each with its own specific rules. From the point of view of political science, however, diplomatic and consular functions both fall within the scope of diplomatic activity as previously defined. We could say, with greater precision, that diplomatic activity *latu sensu* comprises diplomatic activity *stricto sensu* and consular activity. The distinction between the two activities mainly arises out of organizational requirements of the foreign services of each state. Their connection is so obvious that the diplomatic mission can, through consular sections integrated into it, in effect perform all functions considered to be consular, as enshrined in the Vienna Convention on Consular Relations, and consular posts can perform most functions attributed to diplomatic missions by the Vienna Convention on Diplomatic Relations, even if on a smaller and more discreet scale. And consular agents even can, in special cases specified in the former convention, perform diplomatic functions *stricto sensu* (art. XVII).

Thus, we can say that, according to these Conventions, the constitutive elements of diplomatic activity are the following: a) representation; b) protection; c) information; d) promotion; e) negotiation; f) extension abroad of public services. However, not all of these elements have an essential character. Thus, diplomatic activity cannot be conceived without the elements of representation, information, and negotiation. A form of diplomatic activity restricted to these three elements is perfectly possible, but on the other hand, no diplomatic activity is possible without any one of these three elements. The other three may or may not be present according to circumstances, and we therefore consider them accessory, which does not mean they cannot be important in certain cases. If, for example, there are no citizens of country B in country A and if there are no tourist or other kinds of flows between them, the extension abroad of public services of country B in country A will have no interest at all. The same can be said, in certain circumstances, of protection and promotion. On the contrary, if there is in country A a large colony of country B's citizens, even if the political, economic, and cultural links between them are few, the extension abroad of public services of country B in country A will certainly be of major importance. It is also obvious that permanent missions to international organizations will not deal with the extensions abroad of public services.[1]

Summing up, and taking into account the distinction made above, we will group the elements constitutive of diplomatic activity in the following fashion:

a) Representation

b) Information

c) Negotiation

d) Promotion

e) Protection

f) Extension abroad of public services

REPRESENTATION

When representational activities are mentioned in the context of diplomacy, some people immediately think of social or mundane events. However, in a general sense, representation means "acting on behalf of," or in other words, "acting in substitution for someone," without necessarily involving the juridical responsibility of the represented person or organ. Representation as a constitutive element of diplomatic activity—

the sense in which we use the word—is more than representation of a country in social events and less than representation taken in the highly general sense mentioned above. Taken
in this latter sense, all the activities of a diplomatic agent
could be fitted under the heading of representation, that is,
acting on behalf of the represented state in the most diverse
circumstances. Thus, it is not surprising that when the definition of the functions of diplomatic missions was being drafted
in the Vienna Conference on Diplomatic Relations, the argument was made that representation should not be included as
a separate function on a par with others, since all of them
could be included in the general representational function of
the diplomatic agent.[2]

Representation as an element constitutive of diplomatic activity is defined as the set of acts of a diplomatic agent that
have a purely representational character, that is, simply af-
firm the presence or the commitment of the state he or she is
acting on behalf of.

Beyond the representation of a country in social events,
namely in official receptions or banquets or at private events,
diplomatic representation includes the presence of the diplomatic agent in innumerable official acts in which the receiving state requires or expects the presence of diplomatic representatives accredited to it, such as the inaugurations of
parliamentary sessions, the swearing in of heads of state, national funerals, military parades, national day ceremonies, and
solemn inaugurations with the presence of the head of state
or government. On the other hand, in certain circumstances,
the diplomatic agent must speak on behalf of his country and
even commit his state vis-à-vis the authorities of the state to
which he is accredited. This capacity of the diplomatic agent
to commit his country should not be confused with the negotiating function, since the latter, as we will see, consists of a
discussion or debate, the states committing themselves only
to what has been agreed at the end of the negotiation. Conceptually, to negotiate and to commit are two distinct functions.

There was a time when law experts discussed the problem
of whether the chief of a diplomatic mission represented the
head of state of the sending state, or its government, or the

sending state itself. The idea that the chief of a diplomatic mission represented the person of the head of state was certainly a reminder from the time when the power of kings was personal, an idea which is unacceptable since the democratization of the modern state. The Havana Convention on Diplomatic Officials, of February 2, 1928, already mentioned in the preamble that "diplomatic officials do not in any case represent the person of the Head of State but rather their Government." The Vienna Convention on Diplomatic Relations states, with greater propriety, that "the functions of a Diplomatic mission consist, among others, in a) representing the sending State in the receiving State" (art. III). International law experts generally maintain nowadays that the chief of the diplomatic mission represents the state that accredits him to another state. Political science can only support this conclusion, since in the light of pure political theory, the representative function of the diplomatic agent cannot be understood otherwise.

We should note that British ambassadors continue to be called (or to call themselves) "ambassadors of Her Britannic Majesty," and there are authors, albeit not experts, who maintain that British ambassadors represent abroad the person of their sovereign.[3] But in fact, this is but a traditional designation devoid of content in light both of international and British constitutional law.

Concerning permanent missions to international organizations, their representational activities are certainly fewer than those of bilateral missions, but they are nonetheless an important part of the activity of multilateral diplomacy. Regarding the aspect of representation consisting of committing the sending state, it can happen that in some international organizations where the pace of events is highly dynamic, this representational function can be very intense and greater than that of certain bilateral missions.

INFORMATION

Informing is one of the main activities of the diplomatic agent. It is a vast activity whose limits are traced only by the interest or need of the sending state in finding out about certain aspects of the life of the receiving state.

The diplomatic agent accredited to a given country has available to him a great deal of information about the most varied aspects of that country's life, which he may collect, select, analyze, and send to headquarters. Given the huge amount of information and, in many cases, its specialized nature, the most important diplomatic missions generally have specialized personnel to deal with specialized information, namely military, commercial, cultural, and press and other attachés.

Diplomatic information properly speaking is information collected by lawful means. This is a fundamental principle which is part of the very essence of diplomacy and is also enshrined in international law. In effect, the Vienna Convention on Diplomatic Relations estalishes (in art. III, paragraph d) that among the functions of a diplomatic mission is that of "ascertaining *by all lawful means* conditions and developments in the receiving State and reporting thereon to the Government of the sending state."

However, as we already mentioned, deviations from normal diplomatic activity exist, one of them being the gathering of information by unlawful means, euphemistically called clandestine collection, meaning, of course, espionage. This clandestine activity is generally performed by special agents who sometimes enjoy diplomatic cover so as to be able to better and more securely go about their business. Thus, in the diplomatic missions of the most important powers, there are agents accredited as diplomats who, in fact, are intelligence and counter-intelligence agents. In certain, but relatively rare cases, true diplomatic agents also deal with clandestine collection of information.

If the practice of performing intelligence and counter-intelligence operations under cover of diplomatic status has obvious advantages for the countries that use it, it also has certain drawbacks, namely that of somewhat discrediting all diplomatic agents of these countries, because it is often impossible to know whether one is dealing with a genuine or false diplomatic agent. For secret agents posted in more or less democratic countries, it is possible to imagine other covers; but in the socialist dictatorships there are practically no alternatives to diplomatic cover.

However, it should be clear that not all information refering to defense matters or to military strategy collected by intelligence agencies is obtained by clandestine or unlawful methods. The great majority of information gathered by these agencies through their agents abroad is collected by perfectly lawful means. American experts estimate that in open or democratic societies, only 5 percent to 10 percent of collected information has a clandestine origin; in closed or nondemocratic societies, that percentage is 10 to 20 percent.[4]

This fact raises the delicate problem of knowing exactly what can or cannot be considered espionage in a given country. Thus, for example, most countries publish telephone books that are available to everyone, because their aim is to inform the public. A minute analysis of these telephone books can, however, reveal important facts or give valuable hints of a strategic nature. Thus, for example, the sudden appearance in a certain place of a considerable or unusual number of military officials and scientific experts can denote the presence close by of an important military or scientific installation of strategic importance. However, we will not deal with this kind of problem and with others related to the collection and analysis of strategic information, since they are highly specialized matters outside the field of interest of this book.

Diplomatic information, properly speaking, is, as we saw, of a varied nature, and it can be great in quantity, requiring many people simply to collect it. Apart from specialized information (military, economic, scientific, cultural), which is generally dealt with by experts, the diplomatic agents are charged with gathering essentially political information, which is then reported to headquarters by the chief of mission, or at least subscribed by him.

Although this book is not meant to be a guide to diplomatic activity or to indicate a line of conduct, but rather tries to analyze concepts and to build a coherent system with them, we consider it appropriate to analyze the methods generally used by chiefs of mission to analyze and report political information.

Many chiefs of mission, for fear perhaps of seeming to lack zeal and activity, or maybe because they are simply lazy, or because they are devoid of analytic skills, bombard headquarters with a routine flow of information that in great part is copied directly from the daily press.

Regarding this last aspect, it is appropriate to point out at once that summarizing in cables the daily news carried by the press is a waste of time that reveals a great ignorance of journalistic methods and especially of the working of wire agencies. Almost all diplomatic headquarters receive daily the cables of international news agencies, which are simultaneously sent to the newspapers. What the newspapers print, therefore, is not, as a rule, news to headquarters. The chiefs of mission whose cables persistently repeat the daily news carried by the press are not performing a useful task, and, instead of improving their image, are impairing it. This is true, of course, despite the fact that certain editorials or news analyses (not simply daily news) carried by certain newspapers deserve to be quickly transmitted, in part or in full, to headquarters.

Concerning in particular the quantity of news regularly sent to headquarters by chiefs of mission, it must be borne in mind its very abundance can also be a drawback, since a huge flow of information may end up unread even by those for whom it is meant, with the result that when the chief of mission has truly important information to relay, it risks passing unnoticed amid the usual verbiage.

We will recall an observation once made about this matter by Winston Churchill, who, as British prime minister during World War II, replaced Anthony Eden in the Foreign Office when the latter was travelling. In a memorandum to the Secretary-General of the Foreign Office, Churchill said in his polished style:

The zeal and efficiency of a diplomatic representative is measured by the quality and not by the quantity of the information he supplies. He is expected to do a good deal of filtering for himself, and not simply to pour out upon us over these congested wires all the contradictory gossip which he hears.[5]

Still, it is worth mentioning the opinion of Lord Trevelyan, a respected and experienced British diplomat who used to give the following advice: "Draft telegrams as if you were going to have to take them to the local post and pay for them yourselves."[6]

Information sent by the chief of mission should therefore be concise, highly selective, and honest, that is, without subterfuges of false assertions meant to strengthen his credibility or advance his interests. I recall, by the way, the case of a chief of mission whose cables usually began with the sacramental words "an authorized source" or a "a reliable source," whereas at headquarters the source was perfectly known to be his driver. Information must be honest to be taken into due account. And credibility is like virginity: once lost, always lost.

Another delicate problem concerning information is the temptation into which some diplomats fall of relating only what they think will please their governments. Trevelyan said about this: "In diplomatic practice, the mortal sin is to report what the ambassador thinks his government would like to hear."[7]

A well-known American diplomat says, "To report what the State Department wants to hear is still a temptation to American diplomats. Especially in critical times, when both the public and the officials are prey to their emotions, it still requires courage to report unpopular truths which may set the State Department's teeth on edge."[8]

Still another temptation for the diplomatic agent in this field of reporting is that of manipulating information to avoid contradicting or denying points of view or forecasts previously made by him. Acknowledging one's errors by fairly and fully transmitting the facts that show them to be errors also requires courage, awareness of the public interest, and professional integrity.

The diplomatic agent must, of course, send information to the department he serves abroad with exactitude and without important omissions, even if he thus runs the risk of upsetting his hierarchical superiors. This does not mean, however, that he must necessarily adopt an agressive, polemical, or hard-hitting tone, which may cause irritation or even conflict among higher officials. There are ways of transmitting unpleasant news that an experienced and sensible diplomat cannot afford to ignore. However, a great deal depends on the reputation enjoyed by the agent within the department. Statements are allowed to diplomats known for their competence, integrity, and good sense that would be considered intolerable if uttered by an agent with less credit. This element of confidence is not just a condition for the professional success of the agent, but it is also, above all, an essential condition for the regular working of the diplomatic system, which is based on intermediaries. Any diplomatic organization in which the leading posts are occupied by individuals devoid of these three qualities— competence, integrity, and good sense—can be said to have gone astray.

Just as in other careers, there are exceptional diplomats and others less so. In practice, diplomatic agents who, as a rule, do not resist the temptation of reporting only what they think will please their governments or the services on which they depend and who fall prey to the similar temptation of omitting facts that show their previous opinions to be wrong, are naturally those who do not feel secure enough to transmit objectively whatever they know, without fearing the reaction of those to whom their information is addressed. In the short term, this method may produce some favorable results for the agent, but it is generally counter-productive in the long run.

Lastly, there is another aspect of information that must be mentioned to avoid conceptual confusions. We mean not the collection, analysis, and transmissions of information to headquarters, but the diffusion of information about the sending state in the receiving state. This activity of diffusing information about his own country in other countries has nothing to do with the informative tasks of diplomatic agents we are treating now, but rather with the function of promotion with which will be treated later.

NEGOTIATION

The Concept of Diplomatic Negotiation

We already alluded more than once to the idea of international negotiation about which we have advanced the general notion that it consists in contacts between states to arrange the resolution of common or reciprocal interests. We also said that, in a narrower sense, international negotiation would be a discussion between certain states with the goal of reaching an agreement, generally in writing, about any specific problem.

Thus we have before us two concepts of international negotiation. The first is wider in scope, encompassing all the diverse types of contacts between states with the aim of trying to harmonize attitudes or points of views; we may call it informal negotiation, and it constitutes a major part of the normal activity of a diplomatic agent. The second is narrower in scope and concerns contacts between states undertaken through special mechanisms and aimed at reaching agreement, generally in writing, about a specific problem of common or reciprocal interest; we will call it formal negotiation.

International negotiation, whether formal or informal, can be of two types, as we already saw: it can be a negotiation undertaken directly by the holders of political power, which we call direct negotiation; or it can be a negotiation carried out by intermediaries and in this case it is a true diplomatic negotiation. In the present study, we will deal with diplomatic negotiation only. Looked at from a different point of view, we can yet distinguish two kinds of negotiation: bilateral or multilateral, depending on whether the negotiating parties are two or more states.

The American author Fred Charles Iklé defines formal international negotiation as "a process in which explicit proposals are put forward ostensibly for the purpose of reaching agreement on an exchange or on the realization of a common interest where conflicting interests are present."[9] According to this author, there is no room for negotiation in the absence of conflicting interests capable of being resolved by the creation of a common interest.

The French author Alain Plaintey, in a recent book about international negotiation, adopts a definition meant to apply to negotiation in the private sector, given by another French author, L. Constantin. According to this definition, negotiation is "the set of practices that permit the peaceful composition of conflicting or diverging interests of groups or autonomous social entities."[10]

This last definition mentions diverging interests on a par with conflicting interests, which we already deem to be an improvement on the definition mentioned first, which considers that a negotiation always presupposes the existence of conflicting interests. Thus, when two states have only diverging interests concerning a problem or a set of problems, negotiation can be required in the absence of truly conflicting or opposed interests.

Although in the great majority of international negotiations there are opposed or diverging interests, we do not, however, consider the presence or the confrontation of opposed or diverging interests to be an essential element for the definition of international negotiation.

We will give two examples that will help to clarify our point of view.

In the first example, States A and B celebrate a mutual assistance pact that commits them to give each other assistance in case of aggression by a third state against either of them. If we suppose that this agreement has no other clauses but those that establish the mutual obligation of rendering assistance, we see an agreement between two states about a problem of mutual interest, without there being any opposition or divergence of interests.

In the second example, States A and B wish to be elected members of two separate UN committees, and they reach agreement between them to mutually support their candidacies. In this case, there is no opposition of interests between the two states, since each wants to be elected to a different commission. It could be said, however, that they have diverging interests which, by means of a negotiation, are reduced to one reciprocal interest, that is, their mutual support.

By the way, the first example refers to a formal negotiation and the second to an informal negotiation.

As can be seen, neither of our examples fit the definitions given by Iklé and Constantin, but both fit our definition of international negotiation, namely a discussion between states with the aim of reaching agreement about a problem of common or reciprocal interest.

Principles and Methods of Diplomatic Negotiation

The analysis of the principles that rule a diplomatic negotiation and of the methods followed in such negotiations is such a vast and complex matter that an entire book would be required to fully deal with it. There is no room in the tiny space of a chapter for more than a general approach to the subject, which, however, given its obvious interest, deserves a more profound study.

We should warn the student, however, that although there is a large bibliography about the subject, to our knowledge, no textbook is available that is sufficiently thorough and capable of making a valid synthesis of the theory and experience of the technique of international negotiation in a general form, without special reference to specific situations in the field of international relations. Some existing textbooks of a general nature suffer from theoretical weaknesses and from a bad organization of the material; others have undoubted theoretical value but are based on the analysis of specific situations, treating only particular aspects of negotiation.

Preparing the negotiation. To analyze the principles that rule diplomatic negotiations and the methods followed in such negotiations, we must begin by distinguishing two steps: the preparation and the conduct of the negotiation.

The first important principle to bear in mind in a negotiation is that its preparation is a fundamental or decisive element in its failure or success. Naturally, the more important or complex the negotiation, the greater is the need to prepare it carefully.

The first step in the preparation of a negotiation is the

gathering of information, in order to gain a perfect knowledge of the problem or problems to be discussed, to develop arguments for one's own side, and to have as thorough as possible a knowledge of the interests, points of view, and goals of the other party and of the character of the opposite negotiators.

When the problems to be discussed are complex or highly technical in nature, it is necessary to resort to experts to gather the necessary elements. However, the great progress in information techniques that has taken place allows great speed and thoroughness in the gathering of the necessary information, as long as there is an appropriate organization to provide it and analyze it, which is not always the case.

In gathering the information that will support a given negotiation, it is necessary to take into account not only the preparation of one's own case but also the other party's case, as we have already said. For the negotiation to proceed smoothly, it is highly important to know the goals of the other side and the constraints of varied order to which it is subject. Those who think only of their own reasons and minimize or ignore the other's reasons will seldom be able to imagine the possible solutions or to accept the compromises needed to reach final agreement.

Once the information is gathered, it must naturally be organized and studied in order to formulate a negotiating position. Only then can one's own goal in the negotiation be clearly defined, which is also an essential condition for the success of the negotiation. No international meeting can be said to be a negotiation if both parties do not have clearly defined objectives.

Once the available information is analyzed and the goal of the negotiation is clear, negotiating strategy must be set. The term *strategy* in the context of a negotiation is naturally borrowed from the military sciences, in which strategy is generally defined as "the art of using military force to achieve the objectives set by policy." Opposed to strategy is tactics, consisting of "the art of using weapons in combat with maximum effectiveness." Strategy in a negotiation can be defined as "the organized set of means used to achieve the objectives set for the negotiation," or, more simply, "the general orientation that should be given to a negotiation to achieve the objectives set for it." Negotiating tactics could be defined as "the set of means used by the negotiator during a negotiation."

The definition of one or more objectives of a negotiation is a political task, which should be performed by the political authorities. Negotiating strategy sometimes is also defined by political organs but not necessarily so. It is preferable to leave it up to the negotiator to decide which is the best strategy to gain the objective or objectives set at the political level or at least to design that strategy together with the negotiator.

The adoption of an adequate strategy is also, of course, one of the essential conditions for the success of a negotiation. Going back and forth between several strategies or adopting a contradictory strategy makes the negotiation much more difficult or even impossible because the confusion it provokes in the opposite camp. This does not mean that the adopted strategy cannot be flexible or that it should not be adapted according to circumstances. But any change of strategy should be decided by, or in accordance with, the negotiator, for otherwise it may have negative consequences for the result of the negotiation.

The preparation of the negotiation is complete when the negotiator and his team are appointed. This appointment is naturally made by the holders of political power. The nature of the negotiation and its goal should be taken into account in the choice of the negotiator and his team. The qualities of a negotiator are obviously also an important factor for the success of a negotiation. However, we shall deal with this matter later on.

Conducting the negotiation. When we pass from the preparation to the effective conduct of a negotiation, we must take into account negotiating tactics, that is the ways of acting used by the negotiator to achieve the objective or objectives set for the negotiation at the political level. Negotiating tactics are determined exclusively by the negotiator. The ways of acting in a given negotiation are too tightly linked to the personality of the negotiator to be subject to external orders. Any differences between the holders of political power and the negotiator about the way to conduct the negotiation can only be resolved by the replacement of the negotiator and not by direct or indirect attempts to change his or her negotiating tactics.

Especially when we are dealing with complex negotiations involving a large number of participants, the need to organize the negotiation raises numerous tactical problems, which can range from the shape of the negotiating table to the drawing up of the agenda.

In important and difficult negotiations, great care must be taken in drawing up the agenda, since the approval of a given agenda can imply the acceptance of certain principles, not always obvious, or the acceptance of a given orientation desired by the opposition, which may be advantageous to it in the course of the negotiation.

Agendas should be clear and extremely succinct. An excessively long or detailed agenda can raise numerous problems and can even lead to anticipating the discussion of certain points, thus subverting the very purpose of agendas. Another advantage of succinct agendas is that they permit more flexibility in the matters to be discussed. The rigidity of an agenda is directly proportional to its detail.

The flexibility or rigidity of an agenda is also connected to the question of knowing whether, once it is approved, it should be rigorously followed or whether it can be changed in the course of the negotiation. In principle, it is obvious that an agenda that has been discussed and approved should be respected. The question remains, however, whether or not it can be changed because of unforeseen circumstances or as a result of certain conclusions reached during the negotiation. The answer is that if an agenda was drawn up and approved by agreement, it can also be changed by agreement. However, in practice, we must distinguish between the agendas for bilateral and multilateral negotiations. In a bilateral negotiation, with the participation of only two parties, it is not difficult in certain circumstances to reach agreement about a change of the previously accepted agenda. In a multilateral negotiation, however, it is rarely possible to reach agreement on a change of agenda, especially if many parties participate in the negotiation.

On the other hand, even in a bilateral negotiation, if one of the parties refuses to accept a change in the agenda, the change cannot occur. In that case, each negotiator is faced with a dilemma: the party who does not accept a change in the agenda will have to choose between accepting it after all or interrupting the negotiation and the party who wants to change the agenda must choose between letting go of the desired change or interrupting the negotiation. In that case, both parties must carefully weigh the interests at stake in order to reach a decision that will allow the negotiation to continue.

Agendas can be drawn up that foresee the possibility of change or extension, as for example with the inclusion of an item called "other business" or even with reference to the possibility of one of the parties raising any other point not explicitly contemplated in the agenda. But, in a negotiation, whenever a new issue or problem is raised, as foreseen by such an item, the other party or parties can always refuse to discuss it by alleging lack of preparation. If such clauses are conceivable in conferences or international meetings that are not negotiations proper, it is difficult to accept them in true negotiation; even if they are included in the agenda, their effectiveness is doubtful.[11]

Once the agenda is approved, the conduct of the negotiation must be expeditious. All measures that can be taken to shorten the discussions, to keep them within proper limits, and to reject everything that is irrelevant to the negotiation will contribute to its success. Long and repetitive statements, with considerations of little relevance for the resolution of the problems at hand, can only serve to create confusion, to unnecessarily prolong discussions, and to make the identification of the adequate solutions more difficult. An excessively drawn out and confused negotiation is a negotiation in danger of breaking down.

Other important pinciples that must be taken into account in the conduct of a negotiation are negotiating in good faith, avoiding falsehoods, using courtesy, keeping calm in all circumstances, and creating a favorable atmosphere between the negotiating teams.

Good faith in a negotiation can be expressed in several ways. The first, which seems to us the most important, is that which identifies good faith with the will to negotiate, that is to reach agreement about a given problem. There are countries who sometimes accept to negotiate for certain political reasons but do so with the fixed purpose of not reaching agreement. We call this negotiating in bad faith, that is "negotiating without the purpose of negotiating." Another form of good faith is not to conceal the goals one wishes to attain through the negotiation. Yet another is the principle of avoiding any false statements during the negotiation. The use of lies in a negotiation can only led to its failure because it destroys trust between the negotiators, which is a necessary condition to achieve results.

Finally, the success of a negotiation also depends on the existence of a good rapport between the negotiating teams. The participants can create a good rapport by adopting a cordial attitude and always keeping calm, especially when the most difficult and delicate problems come up for discussion. Whatever the value of the arguments being used, the negotiator who never loses his temper around a negotiating table will always gain the upper hand over a negotiator who does and adopts a hectoring tone.

The only exception to this rule is the calculated emotional display aimed at producing a certain effect, since this type of behavior does not spring from uncontrolled emotion but rather is a premeditated and carefully thought-out tactic. It should only be used, however, in exceptional cases, and its use must always be carefully weighed, since it involves the risk of not achieving the desired effect, in which case it is counter-productive.

Beyond these basic principles, which are the material and psychological basis of negotiation, we must deal in greater detail with the very core of negotiation, that is, the way of arguing used by the negotiator, in all its developments and related matters.

The negotiator should use coherent arguments, avoiding any contradictions that can be exploited by his opponent. The arguments should also be clearly and soberly stated in such a way as to avoid irritating or offending the other party or parties. The development of the arguments should always leave

the impression of firmness. Firmness does not mean tough-
ness and is not incompatible with the adoption of a cordial
tone and even with a certain amount of flexibility regarding
the positions that are taken or the proposals that are made.

Inexperienced diplomats or those with little natural ability
for negotiation often confuse firmness with thoughness, provoking the hostility of the opposite party and rendering more
difficult or even impossible the successful conclusion of a negotiation. Conversely, a cordial and calm attitude should not
be confused with weakness. Polite and even-tempered individuals are precisely those who generally prove to be the most
firm negotiators. In Bismarck's famous expression, "Use an
iron hand with a velvet glove."

On the other hand, if the goal of the negotiation is to reach
a compromise between two or more different or opposed positions, flexibility is an essential element of negotiation. By flexibility we do not mean, of course, absence of firmness in the
defense of the interests of one party vis-à-vis the other, but
rather the possibility of moving between the maximum and
minimum objectives to be attained, in order to reach the compromise solution that will permit an agreement between the
parts. Flexibility should also be used carefully, so that any
concession is matched by an equivalent concession.

Negotiations generally progress in a gradual manner, by the
consolidation of certain partial compromises reached in the
course of the negotiation and by setting down the points that
are no longer controversial by the parties, which gradually
leads to a final compromise. As Francis Bacon said: "In all
negotiations of difficulty, a man may not look to sow and reap
at once: but must prepare business, and so ripen it by de-
grees.[12]

The Negotiator

A lot has been written about the qualities of the good negotiator and more still about the qualities of the perfect diplomat. Many of the qualities that are mentioned in these writings are, however, the same qualities needed for the successful
practice of other professions. When it is said, for example, that

a good diplomat must be intelligent, competent, and tactful, the same could be said about a good manager or a good lawyer. Thus, it can be said that a successful negotiator must possess the same qualities that any other successful professional must have, especially those whose activities have a great deal to do with human relationships.

What, in our opinion, can give particular importance to certain human qualities in certain professions and activities is the degree to which they are required for the satisfactory performance of a given activity. Concerning the negotiator in particular, if we must identify a key quality that defines the good negotiator, we would say patience.

François de Callières, who at the beginning of the eighteenth century devoted a profound work to the definition of a good negotiator, after listing several important qualities that he should possess, said the following: "To be successful in this kind of business, he should listen more than he should talk, and he needs calmness, self-control, a lot of discretion and a foolproof patience."[13]

If we should stress another quality of a good negotiator we should say without hesitation that it is the skill to find compromise solutions, which surely sounds vague and even redundant. However, the best way to explain this special skill is to transcribe a remarkable page of Callières's book that describes with impressive accuracy this particular skill of the successful negotiator. Callières says:

Given the fact that state business is usually thorny because of the difficulties of adjusting interests so often opposed between state and princes who do not recognize any judges to their pretensions, one who is charged with such business needs to use his skill to diminish and smooth these difficulties, not only by the expedients suggested by his ingenuity, but also by a flexible and conciliatory spirit that knows how to mold and accommodate itself to the passions, and even to the whims and prejudices, of those with whom he is treating. A difficult man with a crude and antagonizing manner increases the difficulties of the business at hand by the harshness of his character, which irritates and repels the spirit and sometimes transforms trifles and ill-founded pretensions into important affairs, creating obstacles that continuously block the course of the negotiation.

There is a certain dexterity in the art of negotiation, which consists in approaching business from the smoothest side and which an
ancient author (Epictetus) expresses thus: each thing has two han-
dles, one which makes it easier to hold and another which makes if
more difficult. Never try to hold it by the bad handle because you
will then be unable to carry it; take it instead by the other side and
you will carry it easily. The surest way to find the good side is to see
to it that those with whom one is treating notice that it is in their
own interest to accept the proposals made to them, and not simply
to present them by effective reasons; and also, with an agreeable
manner, to concur with their feelings about things not opposed in
essence to the ends to be reached, gradually leading them to a similar concurrence about other, sometimes more important, things.
    . . . Bitter and obstinate arguments with princes and their min-
isters should be avoided, and reasons should be presented to them
without much heat and without always trying to have the last word;
as soon as they begin to boil or become annoyed, it is prudent to
change the subject and to postpone the discussion of the issue at
stake to a better opportunity, which will arise either because the
situation has changed or because the mood has changed, as it always
does because of the natural unevenness and inconstancy of men. A
negotiator must contribute with his manner and with his affability
to put the prince with whom he is treating sufficiently at ease to
listen to and favorably welcome whatever must be told him, which
often depends as much on the manner of saying it as on what it is
said.
    An aggreeable, clear anad enlightened spirit possessing the art of
proposing the most important affairs as if they were easy and advantageous things for the interested parties, and knowing how to do it
with an easy insinuating manner, performs more than half of his
work and finds it easy to conclude it.
    A skillful negotiator should always carefully avoid the stupid van-
ity of trying to seem a shrewd and ingenious man; in order not to
instill mistrust in with whom he is dealing, he must, on the contrary,
try to convince them of his sincerity and good faith and of the integrity of his intentions to compose in a favourable manner the interests
entrusted to him with those of the prince or state to which he is
accredited, which is the true and solid goal to which all negotiations
should aim.[14]

    As can be seen, in a few lucid words, showing a solid expe-
rience and great insight, Callières sums up the qualities of a

talented negotiator, which we gather under the term skill to find compromise solutions.

PROMOTION

We already mentioned that representation, information, and negotiation were essential elements of diplomatic activity. We must now analyze the other, complementary or accessory, elements of diplomatic activity.

We will begin by that element of diplomatic activity which is usually called promotion. As is the case with the other elements already analyzed, promotion can be understood in a very wide sense, in which case practically all diplomatic activity could be included in it, or in a narrow sense, which can be defined as the set of actions undertaken by the diplomatic agent to create or increase a certain type of relations between the receiving state and the sending state. Promotion therefore presupposes initiative and impulse.

Both representation and negotiation can be considered purely passive and routine elements of diplomatic activity. Once the diplomatic agent is accredited to a certain state, he automatically becomes a representative, and his representational activities can be triggered by the initiative of others. On the other hand, the other side can also take the initiative of negotiation, be it formal or informal. Promotion therefore constitutes the dynamic element of diplomatic activity, through which representation is extended, negotiation undertaken or increased in scope, and other elements of diplomatic activity come to life, thus developing relations between states in all fields.

When promotion is mentioned, two aspects of it are generally underlined: the promotion of economic and of cultural relations. This is due to the fact that economic relations and cultural relations are two sectors in which the factor of competition and the need for a specific action by the interested state within other states are felt most acutely. In order to be able to act more efficiently in them, the most important diplomatic missions have experts in these specialized domains. Also for the same reasons, the Vienna Convention on Diplomatic Relations (in art. III), listing the functions of diplomatic missions, singles out concerning promotion the development of "economic, cultural and scientific relations."

It should be added that promotion of the commercial interests of a state within other states is an extremely ancient activity that is connected to the origins of the consular institution. It is likely that ancient Greece kept representatives in Egypt and in other neighboring regions whose functions were very similar to those of modern consular agents. The existence of such agents during the Middle Ages, born of the need created by the intense commercial activity in the Mediterranean basin, is perfectly documented. They not only represented the commercial interests of the various states, but also had the function of arbitrating commercial disputes, which naturally were frequent. The designation *consul mercatorum* that was applied to them hints at this magistrature also contained at first by the consular function.[15]

Finally, we should not forget the important function of promotion in the area of information to which we already alluded. This activity was formerly called propaganda, which, by the way, was an appropriate word, since it comes from the Latin *propagare*, which means diffusing, disseminating, spreading. However, the evil practice of this activity by the totalitarian regimes, particularly during the period prior to World War II, gave the word a pejorative meaning, which led to its improper replacement by the word information, which now designates an activity best called diffusion, which has the same meaning as propaganda.

The word propaganda was first used and adopted to designate the congregation of the Catholic Church created in the sixteenth century to spread the Christian faith through missionary activities among the peoples that did not know Christianity; the congregation was called "for *Propaganda Fide*." However, so-called propaganda activities acquired such a bad reputation in the political field that the Church itself was forced to change the name of that century-old institution, now called Congregation for the Evangelization of Peoples.

This activity of propagating or diffusing information about a certain country in another has, of course, nothing to do with the activities of information of diplomatic agents with which we dealt above, being instead part of the function of promotion that we have been examining.

PROTECTION

If we take the meaning of protection to be, in a highly general sense, the defense of all the interests of the state and its citizens in a given country, the function of protection of diplomats could encompass the whole of their professional activities, as was true also for representation. However, protection as a constituent element of diplomatic activity is understood by us in the restricted sense of the protection of certain specific interests of the sending state and, on the other hand, in the general protection of the citizens of the sending state in the receiving state.

Regarding the specific interests of the state represented by the diplomat, they are fundamentally of two kinds: a) the discharging of the obligations of the receiving state to the sending state; b) the defense of the patrimony of the sending state in the receiving state. State A is committed by agreement to undertake certain actions or to make certain payments to State B. If State A evades its obligations, the diplomatic representative of State B calls on the government of State A to deal with that evasion. On the other hand, State B can have a certain patrimony under its control in State A. The diplomatic representative of State B is in charge of protecting this patrimony. In these various cases, the diplomat therefore performs the function of protecting the rights and specific interests of the representing state in the state to which he is accredited.

But the protective function of the diplomat also includes the protection of the rights and interests of the citizens of the state he represents. This representation is multiple and varied, naturally raising numerous problems of an essentially juridical nature. In a general way, it can be said that the diplomat protects all legitimate personal and patrimonial interests of the nationals of the sending state who live in or are passing through the country where the diplomat performs his or her functions.

Concerning in particular the interests which depend on the local authorities, this protection is necessary only when these authorities are not forthcoming or refuse to recognize the rights of the above mentioned nationals afforded to them by the local legislation or by international agreements. In this case, the intervention of the diplomatic agent is indispensable.

In other situations in which the solution of impending problems does not depend on the local authorities, diplomatic and consular representatives are also forced to intervene to protect the nationals of the state they represent, as, for example, in the cases of repatriation for lack of means of subsistence, or in emergency cases such as may arise due to transportation strikes, robberies, sudden illnesses, public catastrophes, disorders, wars, or civil wars. In all these cases, the diplomatic and consular agent appears clearly in his role of protector of the interests of the citizens of the sending state, and his action is of decisive importance for the effective protection of those interests.

EXTENSION ABROAD OF PUBLIC SERVICE

Another complementary element of diplomatic activity consists in the extension abroad of the public services of a state in the territory of another state through its diplomatic and consular missions.

The citizens of a given state, when they find themselves in the territory of another state, permanently or temporarily, sometimes need access to their national public services in order to exercise their rights or to fulfill their obligations. For this reason, diplomatic missions and consulates are legally authorized to act lawfully on behalf of other public services in the performance for their citizens of certain fundamental public services, such as civil registrar, notarial acts, electoral registration, military draft, and issue of passports and other documents.

Apart from citizens themselves, the transportation carriers of a given state may pass through the territory of another state, requiring the performance of certain formalities in the presence of the official representatives of the country of origin of these transportation carriers. This need first appeared with the passage of ships of a certain state through the harbors of other states, leading to the establishment of consulates in the busiest harbors. Nowadays, with the development of road and aerial communications, the need for an extension abroad of public services for the regular flow of such traffic has increased considerably.

The same is true of the movement of goods between the different states, which sometimes requires the performance of public acts or certain formalities in alien territory by diplomatic or consular representatives.

Today this is a routine matter, which has entered the habits of our civilization and to which generally not much importance is given, but it constitutes nevertheless an important element of diplomatic activity in the general sense of the word.

NOTES

INTRODUCTION

1. *Diplomacy in Modern History*, ed. Laurence W. Martin (New York, London: Macmillan, 1966) p. 1; Raymond Aron, *Guerre et Paix entre les Nations* (Paris: Calmann-Lévy, 1964) p. 141.

2. Hans J. Morgenthau, *Politics Among Nations: The Struggle for Power and Peace* (New York: Alfred A. Knopf, 1978). Morgenthau states in a footnote on p. 146: "By the term 'diplomacy' as used in the following pages, we refer to the formation and execution of foreign policy on all levels, the highest as well as the subordinate."

3. *Peace and War*, ed. Charles R. Beitz and Theodore Herman (San Francisco: W. H. Freeman and Company, 1973).

4. Carl von Clausewitz, *De la Guerre* (Paris: Les Editions de Minuit, 1955) Part 1, Book I, chap. 1, §24, p. 67.

5. *Peace and War*, p. 69. This quotation was taken from Hans Morgenthau or else from the same source used by Morgenthau, who quotes it in the same mistaken form reproduced above (p. 363). The original words of Clausewitz's famous statement, corresponding to the title of paragraph 24 of the first chapter of his famous work are, in effect: "Der Krieg ist eine blosse Fortsetzung der Politik mit anderen Mitteln" (Carl von Clausewitz, *Vom Kriege* [Bonn: Ferd. Dummlers Verlag, 1952], p. 108).

6. Clausewitz, *De la Guerre*, p. 67.

7. Thomas Schelling, "Diplomacy of Violence" in *Peace and War*, p. 75.

8. Garrett Mattingly, *Renaissance Diplomacy* (Baltimore: Penguin Books, 1964).

9. H. Nicolson realized this when he stated in the latter book:

"You may be thinking that in devoting so much space to the new ideas of 1919, I am transgressing my own principle and confusing policy with negotiations, theory with practice." *The Evolution of Diplomatic Method* (London: Constable, 1964, p. 88). George Kennan, a distinguished American career diplomat, called his first book about American foreign policy *American Diplomacy* (London: Secker & Warburg, 1952). In later works about foreign policy, Kennan seems to have understood his error and no longer uses the word *diplomacy* as a synonym of foreign policy. Thus, these works are entitled *Realities of American Foreign Policy, Soviet Foreign Policy*, and *The Cloud of Danger: Current Realities of American Foreign Policy*.

10. Among them is the textbook by K. J. Holsti entitled *International Politics—A Framework for Analysis* (Englewood Cliffs, New Jersey: Prentice-Hall, 1977).

11. In *Approaches to Comparative and International Politics*, ed. R. Barry Farrel (Evanston: Northwestern University Press, 1966), p. 32.

12. Ibid., p. 38.

13. James N. Rosenau, *The Scientific Study of Foreign Policy* (New York: The Free Press, 1971). Chapter 5 of this book is the study mentioned; it is entitled "Pre-theories and Theories of Foreign Policy."

14. R. Aron, *Guerre et Paix entre les Nations* (Paris: Calmann-Lévy, 1964), p. 36.

CHAPTER 1

1. Ragnar Numelin, *The Beginning of Diplomacy* (London: Oxford University Press, 1950), pp. 168–169.

2. *Histoire de la Diplomatie*, directed by Vladimir Potiemkine (Paris: Librairie de Médicis, 1946), Vol. I, pp. 11–16; V. Korosec, *Hethitische Staatsvertrage* (Leipzig, 1892).

3. Potiemkine, *Histoire de la Diplomatie*, p. 16ff; H. Winckler, *Geschichte Babyloniens und Assyriens* (Leipzig, 1892).

4. Chuang Tsze, *Divine Classic of Nau-Hua* (London, 1881).

5. *Lois de Manou*, translated by Elmannovitch, 1913, chap. 7, Roi, 64; quoted in *Histoire de la Diplomatie*, directed by V. Potiemkine, vol. 1, p. 26; K. M. Panikar, *The Principles and Practice of Diplomacy* (Delhi: Ranzit Printers & Publishers, 1952).

6. Judges 11:12.

7. Samuel II 3:12.

8. Kings II 18:19.

9. C. Daremberg, A. Saglio, and E. Pottier, *Dictionnaire des antiquités Grecques et Romaines* (Paris: Hachette, 1873–1919), vol. III, p. 1025.

10. P. Chantraire, *Dictionaire étymologique de la langue grecque* (Paris: Librairie C. Klincksieck, 1974), Vol. 3. The Greek writers of the Roman period, like Polybius (208–126 A.D.) translate the Latin words *legati* and *legatis*—meaning *envoys* and *mission* or *ambassadors* and *embassy*—respectively by *presbeis* and *presbeia*.

11. Daremberg, Saglio, and Pottier, *Dictionnaire*, vol. III, pp. 1027–1029.

12. Thucydides, *History of the Peloponnesian War* (London: W. Heinemann and Harvard University Press, 1965), vol. I, pp. 57–79.

13. Ibid., pp. 109–121.

14. Ibid., p. 121.

15. Harold Nicolson, *Diplomacy* (London: Oxford University Press, 1969), pp. 17–18.

16. Thucydides, *History of the the Peloponnesian War*, pp. 139–141.

17. Ibid., p. 145. Thucydides says about the speeches he mentions: "The speeches are given in the language in which, as it seemed to me, the several speakers would express, in the subjects under consideration, the sentiments most befitting the occasion, though at the same time I have adhered as closely as possible to the general sense of what was actually said" (p. 39).

18. The Latin translations have the title *De falsa legatione*, the meaning which naturally passed over to the European languages. The exact meaning, however, is *embassy in which frauds were committed*, that is, *corrupted embassy*, as can be seen by the French version, translated directly from the Greek and entitled "Sur les forfaitures de l'Ambassade," in Demosthenes, Plaidoyers Politiques (Paris: Les Belles Lettres, 1972), Vol. III.

19. Demosthenes, *Plaidoyers Politiques*, pp. 30–31.

20. Ibid., p. 81.

21. Ibid., p. 82.

22. Harold Nicolson, *Diplomacy*, p. 9.

23. David Jane Hill, *A History of Diplomacy in the International Development of Europe* (London: Longmans, Green and Co., 1921), vol. 1, pp. 11–12.

24. The *Dictionnaire des antiquités Grecques et Romaines*, by Daremberg, Saglio, and Pottier, mentions fourteen different meanings for the word *legatus* (Vol. III, p. 1064).

25. Titus Livius, *Histoire Romaine* (Paris: Les Belles Lettres, 1944). "*Utrimque legati fere*" (Book I, XXII, Vol. I, p. 35; "*Legatos quique ad*

sollicitandum Latium passim dimittunt" (Book II, XXII, Vol. II, p. 33);
"*Aquileiensium legatis*" (Book XLIII, I, Vol. XXXII, p. 2); "*Decernunt
frequentes, ut C. Sulpicius praetor tris ed senatu nominet legatos*"
(Book XVIII, I, Vol. XXXII, p. 3); "*Per idem tempus quinque legati ad
regem missi, qui res in Macedonia aspirecent*" (Book XLII, VI, Vol.
XXXI, p. 53); "*Legatos item mittendos in Africam censuerunt, eosdem
Carthaginem, eosdem in Numidian ad Masinissam*" (Book XXXXI,
IX, Vol. XXI, p. 15)—Cicero, *Correspondence* (Paris: Les Belles Lettres,
1935). "*Crassus tris legatos decernit nec excludit Pompeium*" (XCIV—
A *Lentulus*, Vol. 2, p. 127)—Caesar, *Bellum Gallicum* (Paris: Les Belles
Lettres, 1972). "*Legatos ad Dumnorigem Haeduum mittunt*" (Book I,
IX, Vol. I, p. 8); "*Haedui . . . legatos ad Caesarem mittunt*" (Book 1,
11, Vol. 1, p. 9); "*Legati Helvetti*" (Book I, XIV, Vol. I, p. 11); "*ad Ariov-
istum legatos mitteret*" (Book I, XXXIV, Vol. I, p. 27); "*Mittuntur etiam
ad eas civitates legati, quae sunt citerioris Hispanie finitimae Aqui-
tanie*" (Book III, XXIII, Vol. I, p. 90); "*Legatos ad Caesarem mise-
runt*" (Book VI, XXXII, Vol. II, p. 198); "*Legationis in omnes partes
circummituntur*" (Book VII, LXIII, Vol. II, p. 256); "*Legati ab Ar-
venis*" (Book VII, p. 278); "*Legationibus Remorum*" (Book VIII, VI,
Vol. II, p. 285); "*dimissis nuntiis*" (Book V, XXXIX, Vol. II, p. 158);
"*Dimittit ad finitimas civitates nuntios Caesar*" (Book VI, XXXIV, Vol.
II, p. 200).

26. Titus Livius, *Histoire Romaine*, Vol. II, Book II, XXXIX, p. 59:
"*missique de pace ad Marcium oratores atrox responsun rettulerunt*",
Ovid, *Metamorphosis*, Book IV: "*Ergo tam placidas orator missus ad
aures*"; Virgil, *Aeneid*, Book II: "*Jamque oratores aderant.*"

27. Caesar, *Bellum Galilcum*, Vol. I, Book III, IX, p. 80: "*Legatos,
quod nomen ad omnes nationes sanctum inviolatumque semper fuis-
set, retentos ab se et in vincula coniectos*"

28. Ibid., Vol. I, Book III, XVI, p. 85: "*In ques eo gravius Caesar
vindicandum staluit, quo diligentius in reliquum tempus a barbaris
jus legatorum conservaretur.*"

29. Ibid., Vol. I, Book I, XXXIII–XLVII, pp. 26–40.

30. François C. Ganshof, "Le Moyen Age," in *Histoire des Relations Internationales*, dir. by Pierre Renouvin (Paris: Hachette, 1935),
Vol. I, p. 38ff.

31. Harold Nicolson, *Diplomacy*, p. 20.

32. H. Nicolson says regarding the possibility of being accused of
confusing foreign policy and diplomacy: "The theory of policy and the
theory of negotiation are interactive" (Ibid., p. 17).

33. *De Legatione Constantinopolitana*, Dümmler, Berlin, 1879; idem

ed. G. H. Pertz in Monumenta Germanicae Historica (Hanover: A. Hahniani, 1826–1882), vol. III.

34. Charles W. Thayer, *Diplomat* (Westport, Connecticut: Greenwood Press, 1974), p. 43 and p. 49ff.

35. Mario Oliveri, *Natura e funzioni dei legati pontifici nella Storia e nel contesto ecclesiologico del Vaticano II* (Turino: Marietti), pp. 74–75.

36. Ibid., p. 88.

37. Ibid., page 91ff.

38. Donald E. Queller, *The Office of Ambassador in the Middle Ages* (Princeton: Princeton University Press, 1967) p. 3.

39. Ibid., p. 6.

40. Ibid., p. 28.

41. Ibid., p. 29.

42. Ibid., pp. 42, 46, and 57.

43. Hostiensis, *Summa*, I, *De procuratoribus*, quoted in Queller, *The Office of Ambassador*, p. 59.

44. Queller, *The Office of Ambassador*, pp. 61–62. Chaucer's reference can be found in Troilus and Criseyde, IV, 145: *Thambassiatours hem answerd for final.*

45. *Sexti Pompei Festi De Verborum Significatu. Quae supersunt cum Pauli Epitome*, (Leipzig: Wallace M. Lindsay, 1913), p. 4: *Ambactus apud Euniun (Ann. 601) Lingua Gallica servus appelatur.*

46. Caesar, *Bellum Gallicum*, Vol. II, Book VI, XV, p. 187: *"Ita plurimos circum se ambactos clientesque habet".*

47. E. Littré, *Dictionnaire de la langue française* (Paris: Hachette, 1873) *ambassade*. See also *The Oxford English Dictionary*, vol. I (*embassy*).

48. *Lex Salica*, Tit. I, §4: *Si in dominica ambaxia fuerit occupatus*; Tit. 10, add. 1: *Si eum aut infirmitas aut ambaxia dominica detinuerit*. In S. F. Niermeyer, *Mediae Latinitas Lexicon Minus* (Leiden: E. S. Brill, 1976).

49. *Monumenta Germanicae Historica, Diplomata Karolinorum*, T. I, no. 150: *Escambaldus ad viceen Radoni recognovi et subscripsi. Fulradus ambaxiavit*. In Ibid.

50. In Charles du Fresne Du Cange, *Glossarium mediae et infimae latinitas*, 1883–1887, quoted in Queller, *The Office of Ambassador*, p. 60.

51. *Monumenta Germanicae Historica, Scriptores*, VII, pp. 186, 205, and 212; Einleitung, p. XXVIII, quoted in Queller, *The Office of Ambassador*, p. 63.

52. Bernard du Rosier, *Ambaxiator breviloqus prosaico moralique dogmate pro felice et prospero ducato circa ambaxiatas insistencium excerptus*, in Wladimir E. Hrabar, *De legatis et legationibus tractatus varii* (Dorpat: 1906), pp. 3–28.

53. Machiavelli, *Oeuvres Complètes* (Paris: Pléiade, 1952), pp. 1438ff.

54. Mattingly, *Renaissance Diplomacy*, p. 26.

55. Ganshof, "Le Moyen Age," pp. 38 and 120–121.

56. Philippe de Commynes, *Mémoires* (Paris: Les Belles Lettres, 1964), Vol. I, pp. 135–141. The quoted sentence in the original is the following: *"me semble que les grandz princes ne se doyvent jamais veoir, s'ilz veullent demeurer amys"* (p. 141).

57. Ibid., Vol. I, p. 87: *"Et deux grans princes qui se vouldroient bien entre aymer ne se devroyent jamais veoir, mais envoyer bonnes gens et sages les ungs vers les autres, et ceux-là les entretiendroiet ou amanderoient les faultes."* And on p. 66: "Et se doyvent plustot conduyre ses traictiez loing que près."

58. Mattingly, *Renaissance Diplomacy*, p. 55.

59. Ibid., p. 65.

60. Ibid., p. 68.

61. Ibid., p. 68–87.

62. Mario Oliveri, *Natura e funzioni*, p. 117.

63. Mattingly, *Renaissance Diplomacy*, p. 92.

64. Ermolao Barbaro, *De officio legati*, in Hrabar, *De legatis*.

65. Quoted in Mattingly, *Renaissance Diplomacy*, pp. 94–95.

66. Ibid., pp. 119, 125–127.

67. Ibid., pp. 135–136.

68. Ibid., pp. 137–139.

69. P. José de Castro, *Portugal no Concílio de Trento*, Lisbon: União Grafica, 1944), Vol. III, p. 480; G. Mattingly, *Renaissance Diplomacy*, p. 157 and notes 2 and 3.

70. Mattingly, *Renaissance Diplomacy*, p. 148.

71. Ibid., p. 88.

72. Ibid., pp. 181–183.

73. M. de Callières, *De la manière de négocier avec les souverains, de l'utilité des Negociations, du choix des ambassadeurs & des Envoyes, & des qualitez necessaires pour reussir dans ces emplois* (Brussels: Pour la Compagnie, 1716).

74. Harold Nicolson, *The Congress of Vienna* (London: Methuen, 1961), pp. 218–220.

75. G. de R. de Flassan, *Histoire Générale et Raisonnée de la Diplomatie Française* (Paris, 1811) Vol. VI, p. 193; quoted in E. Satow,

A Guide to Diplomatic Practice (London: Longmans, 1958), pp. 29–30.

76. G. E. do Nascimento e Silva, *Convenção de Viena sobre Relações Diplomáticas* (Rio de Janeiro: Ministério das Relações Exteriores, 1967); Adolfo Maresca, *La Diplomazia Plurilaterale* (Milan: Giuffré, 1979).

77. "Open covenants of peace openly arrived at, after which there shall be no private international understandings of any kind." Ray S. Baker and William E. Dodd, eds. *Public Papers of Woodrow Wilson: War and Peace*, New York: Harper and Row, 1927, vol. I, pp. 159–161.

78. Nicolson, *Diplomacy*, p. 43.

79. Thayer, *Diplomat*, p. 69.

80. See Ganshof, "Le Moyen Age," passim. K. J. Holsti refers in passing to the direct communication between ministers for foreign affairs and heads of states but does not deal with this case in a separate category (International Politics—A Framework for, p. 183).

CHAPTER 2

1. See paragraphs 1 to 3 of the Introduction.

2. Morgenthau, *Politics among Nations*, p. 146, footnote; see p. 13.

3. Jacques Chazelle, *La Diplomatie* (Paris: Presses Universitaires de France, 1962), p. 9.

4. Ibid.

5. A. Y. Vishinsky and S. A. Lozevsky, eds., *Diplomatichesku Slovar* (Moscow: 1948–1950) vol. I, p. 570, quoted in Vernon V. Aspaturian, "Internal Politics and Foreign Policy in the Soviet Union," in *Approaches to Comparative and International Politics*, ed. R. Barry Farrel (Evanston, Illinois: Northwesteren University Press, 1966) p. 214.

6. Holsti, *International Politics*, p. 183.

7. Charles de Martens, *Le Guide diplomatique* (Leipzig, 1866), quoted in Satow, *A Guide of Diplomatic Practice* (London: Longmans, 1958), p. 1.

8. Satow, *A Guide to Diplomatic Practice*, p. 1.

9. Callières, *De la manière*, p. 67.

10. Morton Kaplan, "Introduction to Diplomatic Strategy," *World Politics* (July 1952):548.

11. Caesar, *Bellum Gallicum*, Vol. I, Book I, XXXIII–XLVII, pp. 26–40.

12. N. Machiavelli, *Oeuvres complètes*, pp. 1368–1369 and notes 9 and 11, p. 1543.

13. Commynes, *Mémoires*, pp. 66, 87 and 141.

14. Acheson, *Present at the Creation*, pp. 480, 501–502.

15. Ibid., p. 480; Dean Rusk, "The President," *Foreign Affairs* (April 1960):365.

16. George F. Kennan, *The Cloud of Danger: Current Realities of American Foreign Policy* (Boston: Little, Brown, 1977), pp. 48–49.

17. Daremberg, Saglio, and Pottier, *Dictionnaire*, Vol. II, pp. 266–268.

18. Satow, *A Guide to Diplomatic Practice*, p. 3.

19. Ibid.

20. *The Works of the Right Hon. Edmund Burke* (London: J. Dodsley, 1850), Vol. II, *Letters on a Regicide Peace—Letter IV, To the Earl Fitz William*: "So it was at Paris on the Inaugural day of the constitution for the present year. The foreign ministers were ordered to attend at this investiture of the directory;—for so they call the managers of their burlesque government. The diplomacy, who were a sort of strangers, were quite awe-struck with 'The pride, pomp, and circumstance' of this magnetic senate."

21. Salvatore Bataglia, *Grande Dizionario della Lingua Italiana* (Turin, 1971).

22. Caesar, *Bellum Gallicum*, Vol. I, Book III, IX, p. 80.

23. Nicolson, *Diplomacy*, p. 17.

CHAPTER 3

1. H. Nicolson, *The Evolution of Diplomatic Method* (London: Constable, 1954), pp. 73ff; Nicolson, *Diplomacy*, pp. 28ff; Joseph Frankel, *International Politics*, (London: Penguin, 1973), pp. 148–149.

2. Jules Cambon, *Le Diplomate* (Paris: Hachette, 1926), pp. 119–120.

3. George Modelski, in *Principles of World Politics* (New York: The Free Press, 1972), pp. 180ff, opposes traditional and bilateral diplomacy to modern and multilateral diplomacy, considering the former to be outdated.

4. Nicolson, *The Evolution of Diplomatic Method*, pp. 83–85.

5. Cambon, *Le diplomat*, p. 32.

6. Ibid., p. 31.

7. Sampayo, *O Arquivo do Ministério dos Negócios Estrangeiros*, p. 88.

8. Cambon, *Le diplomate*, p. 30.

9. U.S. Senate Committee on Foreign Relations: Hearing: *Test Ban Negotiations and Disarmament, March 11, 1963* (Washington, 1963), pp. 23–24; quoted in Fred Charles Iklé, *How Nations Negotiate* (New York: Kraus Reprint Co., 1976) pp. 132–33.

10. Iklé, *How Nations Negotiate*, p. 133.

11. Adolfo Maresca, *La diplomazia plurilaterale* (Milan: Giuffré, 1979).

12. Philip C. Jessup, "Parliamentary Diplomacy," *Recueil des Cours*, official review from the International Law Academy, vol. 89, 1956, I.

13. G. E. do Nascimento e Silva, *A missão diplomática* (Rio de Janeiro: Companhia Editora Americana, 1971), pp. 187–8.

14. Thayer, *Diplomat*, pp. 251–52.

15. Ibid., p. 253.

16. Ibid.

CHAPTER 4

1. *The Diaries of Sir Alexander Cadogan (1938–1945)*, ed. David Dilks, (London: Cassel, 1971), p. 249.

2. F. I. Kozhevnikov, ed., *Mezhudna rodnoye Pravo* (Moscow, 1957), pp. 281–282; quoted in Vernon V. Aspaturian, "Internal Politics and Foreign Policy in the Soviet System" in R. Barry Farrell, ed., *Approaches to Comparative and International Politics* (Evanston: Northwestern University Press, 1966), pp. 214–215.

3. *Diplomaticheskii Slovar* (Moscow: Public Publisher for Political Literature, 1960) I, p. 466, quoted in Iklé, *How Nations Negotiate*, p. 230.

4. George F. Kennan, "The Sources of Soviet Conduct," *Foreign Affairs* 25 no. 4. (July 1947); reprinted in George F. Kennan, *American Diplomacy 1900–1959* (London: Secker & Warburg, 1952), pp. 110–112. It is also symptomatic that Soviet diplomats, while repudiating the traditional diplomatic uniform, possess, however, a uniform that is very similar to the military uniform, as was the case with Nazi and Fascist diplomats, who also executed a combat diplomacy.

5. Aspaturian, "Internal Politics," pp. 261–226.

6. Lord Vansittart, "The Decline of Diplomacy," *Foreign Affairs*, 28 (January 1950):180.

7. Thayer, *Diplomat*, p. 42; see pp. 34–36.

CHAPTER 5

1. Modelski, *Principles of World Politics*, p. 187.
2. Ibid.
3. Ibid., p. 190.
4. See p. 33.
5. Acheson, *Meetings at the Summit: A Study of Diplomatic Method* (Durham: University of New Hampshire Press, 1958); *Present at the Creation*, pp. 480, 501–502. Dean Rusk, "The President," pp. 81ff.
6. Modelski, *Principles of World Politics*, p. 191.
7. George F. Kennan, *American Diplomacy, 1900–1950* (London: Secker & Wasburg, 1952), pp. 9–11.
8. Thayer, *Diplomat*, p. lx.
9. Georges Seldes, *The Great Quotations* (New York: Lyle Stuart, 1960), pp. 170–171.
10. *The Diaries of Sir Alexander Cadogan*, pp. 398 and 400–401.
11. *The Ambassador's Directory* (Boston: Diplomatic Press, 1981).

CHAPTER 6

1. José Calvet de Magalhães, *Manual Diplomático* (Lisbon: Ministério dos Negócios Estrangeiros, 1985).
2. The proposal was made by the Holy See delegate, then Monsignor Agostino Casarolli, nowadays Cardinal and Secretary of State. See Nascimento e Silva, *Convenção de Viena sobre relações diplomáticas*, pp. 54–55.
3. For example: Geoffrey Moorhouse, *The Diplomats—The Foreign Office Today* (London: Jonathan Cape, 1977), states: "The Ambassador is a man whom protocol has placed abroad as the personal envoy of his monarch" (p. 242). It is certainly not for reasons of protocol only that British ambassadors are sent abroad, and they certainly are more than personal representatives of the queen.
4. Samuel Halpern, "Clandestine Collection," in *Intelligence Requirements for the 1980's Elements of Intelligence*, ed. Roy Godson (Washington, D.C.: National Strategy Information Center, 1979), p. 37.
5. *The Diaries of Sir Alexander Cadogan*, p. 356.
6. Humphrey Trevelyan, *Diplomatic Channels* (London: Macmillan, 1973) p. 88.
7. Ibid., p. 87.
8. Thayer, *Diplomat*, p. 163.
9. F. C. Iklé, *How Nations Negotiate*, pp. 3–4.

10. L. Constantin, *Psychologie de la Négotiation: économie privée* (Paris: P. U. F.) p. 35; quoted in Alain Plantey, *La Négotiation Internationale—Principes et méthodes* (Paris: Centre National de la Recherche Scientifique, 1980), p. 18.

11. See about this matter the remarks by Iklé, *How Nations Negotiate*, pp. 95–99.

12. Francis Bacon, *Essays and New Atlantis* (New York: Walter J. Black, 1942), p. 200.

13. Callières, *De la manière*, p. 33.

14. Ibid., pp. 128–132.

15. Douglas Busk, *The Craft of Diplomacy* (New York: Frederick A. Praeger, 1967), pp. 124–125.

BIBLIOGRAPHY

Acheson, Dean. *Meetings at the Summit: A Study in Diplomatic Method.* Durham: University of New Hampshire Press, 1958.
———. *Present at the Creation.* New York: W. W. Norton, 1969.
Aron, Raymond. *Guerre et Paix entre les Nations.* Paris: Calman-Lévy, 1964.
Aspaturian, Vernon V. "Internal Politics and Foreign Policy in the Soviet Union." In Farrel R. Barry, ed. *Approaches to Comparative and International Politics.* Evanston, Illinois, Northwestern University Press, 1966.
Bacon, Francis. *Essays and New Atlantis.* New York: Walter J. Black, 1942.
Bataglia, Salvatore. *Grande Dizionario della lingua italiana.* Turin, 1971.
Beitz, Charles R. and Theodore Herman. *Peace and War.* San Francisco: W. H. Freeman & Company, 1973.
Busk, Douglas, *The Craft of Diplomacy.* New York: Frederick A. Praeger, 1967.
Cabot, John Moors. *First Line of Defense.* Washington: Georgetown University Press.
Cadogan, Sir Alexander. *The Diaries of. . . .* ed. David Dilke. London: Cassel, 1971.
Callières, M. de. *De la manière de negocier avec les souverains, de l'utilité des Negotiations, du choix des ambassadeurs & des Envoyez, & des qualités necessaires pour reussir dans ces emplois.* Bruxelles: Pour la Compagnie, 1716.
Cambon, Jules. *Le diplomate.* Paris: Hachette, 1926.
Castro, P. José de. *Portugal no Concilio de Trento.* Lisbon: Uniãs Grafica, 1944.

Caesar, Julius. *Bellum Gallicum*. Paris: Les Belles Lettres, 1972.

Chantraire, P. *Dictionnaire étymologique de la langue grecque*. Paris: Librairie C. Klincksieck, 1974.

Chazelle, Jacques. *La Diplomatie*. Paris: Presses Universitaires de France, 1962.

Cicero. *Correspondence*. Paris: Les Belles Lettres, 1935.

Clausewitz, Carl von. *De la guerre*. Paris: Les Éditions de Minuit, 1955.

————. *Von Kriege*. Bonn: Fred. Dummlers Verlag, 1952.

Commynes, Philippe de. *Mémoires*. Paris: Les Belles Lettres, 1964.

Daremberg, C., Saglio, A., and Pottier, E., *Dictionnaire des antiquités Grecques et Romaines*. Paris: Hachette, 1873–1919.

Demosthenes. *Plaidoyers Politiques*. Paris: Les Belles Lettres, 1972.

Farrel, R. Barry, ed. *Approaches to Comparative and International Politics*. Evanston, Illinois: Northwestern University Press, 1966.

Festi, Sexti Pompei. *De Verborum Significatu. Qual supersunt cum Pauli Epitome*. ed. Wallace M. Lindsay. Leipzig, 1913.

Frankel, Joseph. *International Politics*. London: Penguin, 1973.

Ganshof, François D. "Le Moyen Age." In *Histoire des Relations Internationales*. Directed by Pierre Renouvin. Paris: Hachette, 1935.

Godson, Roy, ed. *Intelligence Requirements for the 1980's: Elements of Intelligence*. Washington: National Strategy Information Center, 1979.

Hill, David Jane. *A History of Diplomacy in the International Development of Europe*. London: Longmans, Green and Co., 1921.

Holsti, K. J. *International Politics: A Framework for Analysis*. Englewood Cliffs, New Jersey: Prentice-Hall, 1977.

Hrabar, Wladimir E. *De legatis et legationibus tractatus varii*. Dorpat, 1906.

Iklé, Fred Charles. *How Nations Negotiate*. New York: Kraus Reprint Co., 1976.

Jackson, Geoffrey. *Concorde Diplomacy*. London, Hamish Hamilton, 1981.

Jessup, Philip C. "Parliamentary Diplomacy." In *Recueil des Cours* review of the "Académie de Droit International," vol. 89, I, 1956.

Kaplan, Morton. "Introduction to Diplomatic Strategy," In *World Politics* (July 1952).

Kennan, George F. *American Diplomacy:1900–1950*. London: Secker & Warburg, 1952.

———. *The Cloud of Danger: Current Realities of American Foreign Policy*. Boston: Little, Brown, 1977.

Korosec, V. *Hethitische Staatsvertrage*. Leipzig: 1931.

Lall, Arthur. *Modern International Negotiation*. New York: Columbia University Press, 1966.

Littré, Émile. *Dictionnaire de la langue française*. Paris: Hachette, 1873.

Livius, Titus. *Histoire Romaine*. Paris: Les Belles Lettres, 1944.

Luidprand. *De Legatione Constantinopolitana*. Dümmler. Berlin, 1879; ed. Pertz, G. H., in *Monumenta Germaniae Historica*, Hanover: A Hahoniani, 1826–1882, vol. III.

Machiavelli. *Oeuvres Complètes*. Paris: Pléiade, 1952.

Magalhães, José Calvet de. *Manual Diplomático*. Lisbon: Ministério dos Negócios Estrangeiros, 1985.

Maresca, Adolfo. *La diplomazia plurilaterale*. Milan: Giuffré Editore, 1979.

Martens, Charles de. *Le guide diplomatique*. Leipzig, 1866.

Martin, Lawrence, ed. *Diplomacy in Modern History*. New York: Macmillan, 1966.

Mattingly, Garrett, *Renaissance Diplomacy*. Baltimore: Penguin Books, 1964.

Modelski, George. *Principles of World Politics*. New York: The Free Press, 1972.

Moorhouse, Geoffrey, *The Diplomats—The Foreign Office Today*. London: Jonathan Cape, 1977.

Morgenthau, Hans J. *Politics among Nations: The Struggle for Power and Peace*. New York: Alfred A. Knopf, 1978.

Nicolson, Harold. *Diplomacy*. New York: Oxford University Press, 1969.

———. *The Congress of Vienna*. London: Methuen, 1961.

———. *The Evolution of Diplomatic Method*. London: Constable and Co., 1954.

Niermeyer, J. F. *Mediae Latinitatis Lexicon Minus*. Leyden: E. S. Brill, 1976.

Numelin, Ragnar. *The Beginning of Diplomacy*. London: Oxford University Press, 1950.

Oliveri, Mario. *Natura e funzioni dei legati pontifici nella Storia e nel contesto to ecclesiológico del Vaticano II*. Turin: Marietti, 1979.

Panikar, K. M. *The Principles and Practice of Diplomacy*. Delhi: Ranzit Printers & Publishers, 1952.

Plaintey, Alain. *La négotiation Internationale—Principes et méthodes*. Paris: Centre National de la Recherche Scientifique, 1980.

Potiemkine, Vladimir, et al. *Histoire de la Diplomatie*. Paris: Librairie de Médicis, 1946.

Queller, Donald E. *The Office of Ambassador in the Middle Ages*. Princeton: Princeton University Press, 1967.

Rosenau, James. *The Scientific Study of Foreign Policy*. New York: The Free Press, 1971.

————. *International Politics and Foreign Policy*. New York: The Free Press, 1969.

Rusk, Dean. "The President." *Foreign Affairs* (April 1960).

Sampayo, Luiz Teixeira de. *O Arquivo do Ministério dos Negócios Estrangeiros*. Coimbra: Universidade Imprensa da Univernidade, 1925.

Satow, Ernest. *A Guide to Diplomatic Practice*. London: Longmans, 1958.

Silva, G. E. do Nascimento e. *A missão diplomática*. Rio de Janeiro: Companhia Editora Americana, 1971.

————. *Convenção de Viena sobre Relações Diplomáticas*. Ministério de Relações Exteriores, 1967.

Thayer, Charles. *Diplomat*. Westport, Connecticut: Greenwood Press, 1974.

The Ambassador's Directory. Boston: Diplomatic Press, 1981.

Trevelyan, Humphrey. *Diplomatic Channels*. London: Macmillan, 1973.

Tsze, Chuang. *Divine Classic of Nan-Hua*. London, 1881.

Thucydides. *History of the Peloponnesian War*. London: V. Heineman and Harvard University Press, 1965.

Vansittart, Lord. "The Decline of Diplomacy." *Foreign Affairs*, 28 (January, 1950).

Watson, Adam. *Diplomacy—The dialogue between states*. London: Eyre Methuen, 1982.

Winckler, H. *Geschichte Babyloniens und Assyriens*. Leipzig, 1892.

INDEX

About the Author

JOSÉ CALVET DE MAGALHÃES is a retired Ambassador of Portugal. He is the author of *Diplomatic Manual* (in Portuguese), *History of the Portuguese Economic Thought,* and other works. He is currently at work on a history of the diplomatic relations between the United States and Portugal, and has published articles in *Estratégia—Revista de Etudos Internacionais.*

Recent Titles in
Contributions in Political Science
Series Editor: Bernard K. Johnpoll